Dream
Interpretation
(and more!)
Made Easy

Books by Kevin J. Todeschi

Dream Interpretation (and More!) Made Easy

Edgar Cayce's ESP

The Edgar Cayce Ideals Workbook

Edgar Cayce on the Reincarnation of Biblical Characters

Edgar Cayce on the Reincarnation of Famous People

Edgar Cayce on the Akashic Records

Edgar Cayce on Soul Mates

The Encyclopedia of Symbolism

The Persian Legacy and the Edgar Cayce Material

*Soul Development: Edgar Cayce's
Approach for a New World*

Twelve Lessons in Personal Spirituality

Dream Interpretation

(and more!)

Made Easy

by KEVIN J. TODESCHI

PARAVIEW PRESS

NEW YORK

*To Kurt, Heidi and Kellie
and the dreams of youth we shared.*

Contents

"As we see, all visions and dreams are given for the benefit of the individual, would they but interpret them correctly."

Edgar Cayce, 1925

Introduction

The earliest dreams I remember are from the age of seven. I still recall two with relative ease even now, decades later. Both dreams had a profound effect upon my waking mind and my thoughts during the course of the many days that followed. One of those dreams was a nightmare, the other was a pleasant adventure. The nightmare caused me a great deal of fear and apprehension. The adventure gave me much joy and an excitement that nearly rivaled a child's anticipation of Christmas morning. The nightmare made me afraid to go to sleep, worried that a similar experience might trouble my dreams. The adventure filled me with anticipation when it was time to go to bed, hoping to pick up the story once more – something I actually managed to do on at least six occasions.

These two dreams have stayed with me through the years. If I could speak to myself as a seven-year-old from my present vantage point, I could provide an explanation that would probably set my mind at ease in one case and totally ruin a childhood fantasy in the other. If I had told my parents about either experience, I know that they would have listened but ultimately reassured me that dreams were "only my imagination." After working with dreams for more than twenty-five years and speaking throughout the United States, as well as in seven other countries, I know that children all over the world have heard this phrase. What is not stated, perhaps because it is not generally accepted or known, is that although dreams are pulled together from within the recesses of the subconscious mind – a place we too easily relegate to "only the imagination" – these imaginative wanderings have meaning. By suggesting that the imagination is unimportant in terms of dreams, we are unfortunately negating a wealth of insight, direction and counsel that is easily accessible to every individual.

Having taught hundreds of individuals dream interpretation and spoken to perhaps a thousand more, I know that a frequently asked question is "Do all dreams really have a meaning?" I have come to believe that the answer is simply, "Yes!" To be sure, sometimes that meaning is not very important but every dream has a meaning nonetheless. For example, let's say that a student stays up late at night watching television, speaking with friends or studying and then has the urge for a midnight snack, devouring a pizza just before bed. After falling asleep that individual dreams about a horrendous war, a military conflict, or the explosion of an atomic bomb. You might think that the dream is a prophetic vision of things to come but it is simply suggesting that the individual's digestion is "at war."

Another misperception about dreamwork is that it takes an expert to somehow decipher the substance of dreams. The truth of the matter is that each individual is ultimately the best interpreter of his or her own dreams. Why? Because each of us is aware of the events occurring in our lives, as well as the feelings we hold and the personal relationships we are experiencing with other individuals. These things are readily explored in dreams. Although someone who has experience with dream interpretation can often facilitate the discovery of a possible meaning, it is generally up to the dreamer alone to decide what applies and what doesn't.

In my own life, other than remembering an occasional dream, I really was not actively involved in dreamwork until I became interested in the work of Edgar Cayce (1877-1945). Called the "father of holistic medicine," "the Sleeping Prophet," and "the greatest psychic of the twentieth century," for forty-three years of his adult life, Cayce was able to enter into a self-induced sleep state and provide psychic information, called "readings," to virtually any question imaginable. In addition to subjects such as health, philosophy, spirituality, and psychic ability, much of the Cayce material deals with dreams and dream interpretation. That information first opened up the world of dreams to me and provided a foundation and an understanding that has stood firm for more than twenty-five years.

Edgar Cayce emphasized the importance of working with dreams, stating as early as 1923 that attempting to understand what he called the subconscious, the psychic, and the soul forces of each individual should be "the great study for the human family." The rationale from Cayce's perspective was that through the study of the subconscious and psychic part of ourselves we would come to an understanding of the nature of the soul, our connection to one another and our relationship with the Creator.

Almost nine hundred of the more than 14,000 Cayce readings on file at the Association for Research and Enlightenment in Virginia Beach, Virginia deal with the subject of dreams and dream interpretation. Generally, when Edgar Cayce was asked to discuss the meaning of a dream, his wife would simply hold a copy of the dream in her hand and ask that the dream be interpreted – without the dream itself ever being read! Even more amazing is the fact that on numerous occasions when Cayce was provided with an individual's request for interpretation, he would remind the dreamer of forgotten portions of his or her own dream!

In terms of dream material, one of Cayce's most involved supporters was a wealthy, young Jewish stock broker named Morton Blumenthal who received hundreds of dream interpretation readings for himself as well as for members of his immediate family. Extremely interested in the nature of the soul and each individual's relationship to God, one of Morton's dreams explored this very topic in a humorous vein.

In part, Morton dreamed that he was in his apartment in New York City. Suddenly the doorbell rang and his maid went to answer the door. She announced the presence of a "distinguished visitor" and Morton jumped to his feet in exhilaration with the sudden knowledge that God Himself had come to call. Morton ran up to God and embraced Him with a hug. God's appearance was very business-like. He was clean-shaven and clean-cut, wore an expensive suit and a derby hat. He also seemed strong and intelligent, just the sort of man with whom Morton would like to do business.

Because God was visiting, Morton decided to give Him a tour around the apartment. Things went well enough until Morton realized they were approaching the living room and that he had mistakenly left his liquor cabinet half-open. Understanding that God probably knew everything, Morton decided to reveal everything rather than trying to hide his liquor supply. He flung the cabinet wide open and pointed out the bottles by stating, "In case of sickness." God's reply was matter of fact: "You are well prepared!"

Later, when asked for an interpretation, Cayce stated that much of Morton's dream indicated that each and every individual can have a personal relationship with the Divine. This interpretation becomes obvious when we consider that God comes to meet us in the form that we might best recognize Him, that He comes not as some supreme deity but as someone we might relate to, and that He is extremely accepting of us in spite of our imperfections.

The Cayce information suggests that dreams essentially analyze, compare and contrast the events, thoughts, and issues of each day. Their relevance has physical, psychological, and even spiritual significance. In addition to understanding the nature of the soul and our relationship with God, the benefits of dream exploration include such practical matters as problem solving, understanding relationship and work issues, prophetic voyages, a deeply personal look into self discovery, and the search for meaning. So the reasons for exploring dreams are numerous.

Conversely, in my work with hundreds of individuals, I have found that people offer four excuses for not explored their own dreams: (1) "Dreams don't mean anything," (2) "I don't dream," (3) "I don't know how to interpret them," and (4) "I don't have time to be bothered."

Contrary to the first response, I have personally witnessed countless individuals become puzzled and even amazed by what their dreams revealed about them. Whether it was a personal secret that had not been told to another individual, an issue with which the person had been struggling, or an event that was about to occur, the dreamer was often taken completely by surprise. One of my favorite instances occurred one night during an ElderHostel program where I had been asked to work with a group of conference attendees on the subject of dream interpretation.

ElderHostel is an organization that provides seniors with a variety of educational programs around the country. During this particular event, I was standing in front of an audience of approximately fifty individuals and had just given some background information on dreams and how they worked. I then asked for volunteers from the audience to share any dreams that they would like to have discussed and analyzed. After a moment's hesitation one gentleman of about sixty-five raised his hand. He began by stating, "I have a dream, but it doesn't mean anything." I simply nodded and asked him to relate his dream to the group. The dream seemed to cause his wife, who was sitting next to him, some measure of embarrassment.

In the dream, he found himself on the second floor of a two-story house. He was in the master bedroom in his pajamas. His wife was lying in the bed completely naked, waiting for him. Before getting into bed with his wife, he related that he had suddenly remembered something, although he couldn't consciously remember what that something had been. As a result, in the dream he left his wife and the bedroom and proceeded downstairs to the first floor. He seemed to "putter around" doing something for awhile before suddenly remembering that his wife was upstairs naked in bed and this was his "chance for romance." That thought caused him to retrace his footsteps, but he was surprised and "very frustrated" to find that the stairway to the second floor had suddenly disappeared. That was the end of the dream.

One of the mistaken assumptions regarding the subject of dream interpretation is that each dream should have only one interpretation. This is wrong for a variety of reasons. One is that two individuals might have a similar dream but the interpretation can be very different. Why? Because each individual may have very different feelings or beliefs about the images or events being portrayed in the dream and each may have completely contrasting experiences occurring in their waking lives at the time of the dream. Another reason is that dreams often have multiple meanings, corresponding to the various aspects of the individual as well as her or his physical, mental and spiritual self. Keeping these factors in mind, I attempted to analyze the man's dream by diplomatically suggesting that sometimes a dream like this might indicate that their was some kind of a sexual issue or problem. Obviously a dream of this nature – a husband not being able to have sex with his wife – could be interpreted in this manner.

After my suggested "possibility," the dreamer emphatically rejected any such idea, insisting, to his wife's red-faced embarrassment, that there had "never been a problem and never would be a problem." When the ElderHostel group had stopped laughing, I then offered a second interpretation: "Do you have the habit of starting projects that you never really follow through on, which is causing a great deal of frustration to members of your household?" The dreamer looked at me in complete confusion, but his wife began nodding her head in total agreement. She then volunteered the fact that "Even now he has the beginnings of a deck out back that he has been working on for six months and still hasn't gotten around to finishing." I thought this interpretation was likely because in this instance the house could represent his "current situation," the wife that he doesn't make love to "something that he doesn't follow through on," and his own emotion of being frustrated "a likely feeling being experienced by someone within his environment."

The second reason individuals give for not exploring the topic of dream interpretation is, "I don't dream." Scientific studies have proven otherwise. In a 1953 article in the journal Science, Eugene Aserinsky and Nathaniel Kleitman of the University of Chicago, discussed for the first time their findings that REM (rapid eye movement) sleep indicated dream periods. Their discovery led to countless scientific investigations of the same topic. As it turns out, dreams are not necessarily limited to REM sleep but rapid eye movements can be a major determinant in indicating the possibility that a dream is taking place. It is now believed that most individuals dream a number of times each night, for a total of ninety minutes or more on average.

So it is not so much a lack of dreams, as it is individuals not bothering to reflect upon their dreams when awakening, let alone attempting to record them. Because dreams are the substance of the subconscious mind, they are extremely fragile, illusive, and easily dissolved by the intrusion of waking consciousness and the left brain. Often, students have told me how they have awakened from sleep, aware of the presence of a dream but that as soon as they attempted to put all the pieces together and "remember the whole story," the dream disappeared. A better approach is simply to begin writing down whatever is on the verge of consciousness immediately upon awakening. Even if the dreamer only remembers a feeling, a color, or a specific character or place, they should write it down. With this approach, individuals will often find that more pieces fall into place as they are writing and dream recall becomes not so much a goal of remembering but a process of re-experiencing.

The third reason individuals give to explain their hesitation in undertaking an examination of their own dreams is, "I don't know how to interpret them." But I repeatedly tell people that interpretation is not a skill so much as it is a process. It is more important to simply become comfortable with the dream interpretation process. Individuals also need to keep in mind the fact that they already know the possible meaning of many more symbols than they might consciously be aware. However, they need not memorize the meanings of hundreds of symbols. These meanings can be discovered in a variety of ways – by using a good dream dictionary, an unabridged dictionary, one's own logic, or even asking friends to brainstorm possibilities. What is more meaningful is becoming comfortable with the dream interpretation process.

Many dream symbols are actually quite easy to interpret. For example, most people know that bad luck can be symbolized by a black cat, walking under a ladder, or breaking a mirror. Conversely, good luck might be indicated by such things as a rainbow, a four-leaf clover or finding a genie's lamp. Places also lend themselves to interpretative meaning: A library suggests knowledge, a post office suggests communication or a message, and a church suggests spirituality. Most individuals could easily decipher each of these symbols.

In addition to their usual meanings, words have a variety of metaphorical meanings that lend themselves to symbolism. A fish might suggest something's fishy; a book could indicate a regulated process of playing by the book; and, a forest might show that an individual is so caught up in details that she or he can't see the forest for the trees. Metaphors often present themselves in a variety of ways in dreams.

Dream interpretation is something that virtually everyone can accomplish. After working with thousands of dreams, I have come to believe that dreams might be considered "a right-brained process" whereas their interpretation is perhaps best undertaken with logic and "a left-brain approach."

One dream student who told me that she did not know how to interpret her dreams related the following example: She dreamt that she saw her brother in her backyard. He was standing next to a compost pile with a rake in hand, as though he had been gathering some of the material together. To the dreamer's surprise, a telephone sat on top of the pile of compost. When I asked the dreamer if she was having problems communicating with her brother, she looked at me in compete astonishment and inquired, "How did you know?" I explained to her that one possibility suggested by the imagery was simply that her communication (telephone) with her brother (who appeared in the dream) was rotten (compost pile), and that he had been trying to work (rake) on the situation, whereas she had not. After my explanation the dreamer could clearly see how I had arrived at the interpretation from the images provided in her dream.

A final reason individuals give for not working with their dreams is, "I don't have time." In response to this statement, I often ask people to consider what they might do if they lived with one of the greatest counselors, psychics, or advisors of all time. Wouldn't they want to check in at least occasionally for advice, counsel or personal encouragement? Ignoring the deeper substance of a meaningful dream is like deciding not to open a letter from a trusted and close personal friend. Why would individuals not want to hear from someone who loves them unconditionally, knows them intimately, and only wants what is best for them? No one knows an individual and his or her life better than that person's subconscious mind. At this level, each and every one of us is much more in touch with ourselves, our surroundings, and our personal lives than we could possibly be aware.

If I could speak to myself as a seven-year-old and explain why I had dreamed that a hideous monster had come to fetch me, I would say that it was simply in response to my having taken something that did not belong to me from a neighborhood child. The guilt had begun to devour me. Even though I was not aware of the dream's meaning, shortly thereafter I returned the rubber-band gun I had taken. My dream of being with a girlfriend that I did not really have (who somehow made my life complete) turned out to be partially prophetic. More than twenty years later I met and married a woman very much like the one portrayed in the dream. The dream was simply a response to my loneliness at the time and my feeling like an outcast with regards to my peers. It was also a subconscious prompting to incorporate the various aspects of my being, and to learn to like myself so that I could truly like and have relationships with others.

Although I have learned a great about dreams from working with other people, perhaps more importantly I have learned a great deal about myself and how to show others how they can do the same. This book is written in the hope that it might make some small contribution to a day somewhere off in the future when each and every individual is encouraged to work with dreams as a normal part of everyday life, and when no child is ever again told that a dream is "only your imagination."

CHAPTER 1

Interpreting with symbolism

As long as there have been human beings, there have been dreams. Dreams date back millions of years. Whether our ancient ancestors regarded dreams as messages from the gods, omens, or simply extensions of daily life is subject to much conjecture. What is known is that the evidence of our fascination with dreams dates back to the first written words.

One of the earliest indications of dream interpretation comes from Egypt in the form of the Chester-Beatty papyrus. Perhaps the oldest "dream dictionary" in existence, this 4,000-years-old document contains a number of dream symbols and their possible corresponding meaning. For example, to the early Egyptians, dreaming about seeing one's bed on fire could represent the rape of one's wife, whereas dreaming of looking at a snake might signify abundance. Although they do not necessarily have the same meaning today, both of these are examples of cultural symbols, which I will discuss later.

For eons, many cultures believed that God literally spoke to His human children through their dreams. With this in mind, it is no wonder the Bible contains approximately seventy-five references to dreams throughout the Old and New Testaments, including the Creator's announcement that "If there be a prophet among you, I the Lord will make myself known unto him in a vision, and will speak unto him in a dream" (Numbers 12:6). In early Judaism, symbols such as the rainbow, the rite of circumcision, and a recognition of the Sabbath were signs that signified the mystical relationship between God and humankind. The rabbinical contributions to the Talmud also contain hundreds of references to dreams and the logical connections between symbolism and consciousness. As one example, according to the Talmud, salt symbolizes the Torah because just as the world cannot exist without salt, it cannot exist without the Torah.

The Greeks also placed much significance on the ability of dreams to relate important information to the dreamer. During the Greco-Roman period, dream incubation, which enabled individuals to obtain guidance from the gods, was a common practice. At the temple of Asclepius, the Greek god of healing, patients attempted to dream for information that would enable them to recover from the ailment that troubled them. Temple priests were on hand to assist dreamers in interpreting whatever guidance came their way.

It is also from the Greeks that we get the word symbol, derived from "symbolon," which means an insignia or a means of identification. In simplest terms, a symbol is a visible representation of an object or an idea. A word or an image is symbolic when it implies something more than its obvious and immediate meaning. Symbols provide mirror images of feelings, situations, fears, experiences, needs, potentials, and desires.

The interpretative meaning assigned to symbols is not a random definition to be memorized, but a logical connection that the dreamer can usually discover. In other words, a symbol does not mean something simply because a meaning for it is listed in a dream dictionary; invariably there is a rational explanation. For this reason, dreamers oftentimes have an "Aha!" experience when a possible meaning for their dream is discussed – generally the meaning becomes apparent and is not simply a matter of conjecture. Certainly this was the experience of a thirty-year-old Navy wife who related the following dream:[1]

> *I dreamed that my husband, Bill, and I were on a little bitty island (like in the cartoons) in the middle of the ocean. The dolphins were swimming by and the water was beautiful just like the island of Guam, from which we recently moved. I was watching the dolphins when suddenly Bill jumped in the water.*
>
> *Before I could do anything I saw a killer whale. I was afraid to get in the water and I couldn't see Bill. I was scared because I thought I had lost him. Then this huge killer whale jumped out of the water onto the little island. Its head had a huge hole*

---

[1] Each of the dreams used within this volume is real, although the names have been changed to maintain confidentiality

*in it as if it had eroded from toxic waste or something. I started
to cry. I wanted to help it but I was afraid to get close.*

*The whale knew what I was feeling and started flapping
these things inside its head and I understood perfectly what it
was saying to me. It was as if we could read each other's minds
because no words were spoken. It was telling me that its sore
didn't hurt and not to worry because the missing skin would
grow back. It then told me that if I wanted to go find my husband I could ride on its back.*

*The whale stated that although we (the whale and I) had a
hard time communicating, we would be able to understand one
another and everything would be okay. The whale had a big
smile and a beautiful laugh that made me smile as well. I
remember feeling guilty for being human and allowing bad
things to happen to these beautiful animals but I felt so good
when the whale seemed to forgive me.*

Although the woman first expressed total confusion regarding the
possible meaning of her dream, it only took a few insights to lay the
groundwork for her understanding. I pointed out that the whale seemed to
symbolize her husband. The rationale was two-fold: The whale had not
appeared until after her husband's disappearance, and in the dream she had
also expressed that she was having a hard time communicating with this
creature even though there was obviously deep affection between them.
The fact that the whale had a "toxic waste" sore on his head suggested to
me that her husband had been constantly worried or concerned about
something that was basically eating away at his thoughts.

Continuing my observations, I thought that the island represented
their life together. Although her husband appeared content with the tiny
world within which they lived (the cartoon island), she was looking for
broader horizons. In this dream the dolphins might indicate an interest in
spirituality. When I inquired as to whether she and her husband were argu-
ing about their life situation – she wanting more and he not understanding
why – the dreamer expressed total agreement with my assessment.

According to the dreamer, she and her husband had just moved back
to the United States. In the process of moving, she had decided to give up
her career in administration and pursue "something more meaningful."

Her interests turned to holistic health and spirituality. She returned to school to get a job as a health care practitioner. From her husband's perspective, this change in his wife had been the cause of much concern: "My husband is a man of few words but I knew all my talk of holistic healing was driving him a little crazy. He wanted me to have a paycheck every two weeks and continue to be 'normal.'"

The dreamer confessed her fear that she had begun to worry that her beliefs and her desires for the future were so different from his that she and her husband would begin to grow apart. She was relieved to see that the dream suggested otherwise. Although it had been difficult to communicate with the whale, the dream ended with the knowledge that they "would be able to understand one another and everything would be okay."

After the initial "Aha!" experience, dream interpretation students often ask questions like: "Why do dreams have to be interpreted anyway?" or "Wouldn't it be easier if the unconscious mind just told me what it wanted me to know in plain language?" This is an extremely common inquiry for individuals beginning to pursue the meaning of their dreams. Perhaps the best answer is that the language of the brain is symbols; it is not any spoken language. For this reason, individuals can often help one another with dream interpretation even when they might not be able to communicate in the same verbal language.

I have been able to assist individuals with their dreams in places like Japan, France, South America, Egypt, Greece, Israel – literally all over the world. Although our ability to communicate verbally may be limited, each of us shares the language of symbols because it is connected to the nature of our consciousness. For contributing to this very understanding, we owe a debt of gratitude to two pioneers in the field of psychology, Sigmund Freud and Carl Jung.

The founder of psychoanalysis, Sigmund Freud (1858-1939) was a pioneer in exploring the unconscious and dreams. Although many now regard Freud's work on dreams as somewhat limited in perspective, he is often credited with generating a modern-day interest in dreamwork. To be sure, Freud was not the first scientist to explore the topic of dreams, but his book *The Interpretation of Dreams* (1899) laid the groundwork for a great deal of dream analysis that followed.

Essentially, Freud assumed that dreams are not a matter of chance but are instead *associated* with conscious thoughts and problems. In his approach, dreams are the unconscious mind's expression of deeply rooted experiences and even traumas. This idea was based in part on earlier studies that recognized the symbolic meaning of some neurotic psychological symptoms. For example, physicians had previously identified such problems as psychological asthma, in which one feels stifled or unable to breathe, and eating disorders, in which one feels as though she or he cannot eat, swallow, or accept something.

Through a technique Freud called "free association," individuals would repeatedly discuss their dream images and thoughts until they reached the unconscious core of what the dream was really about. The dream itself was the manifest content whereas the unconscious prompting that had created the dream was known as the latent content. In this view, the nature of the conscious mind could be regarded as the tip of an iceberg: the conscious mind is only a portion of the whole mind. The rest exists below the surface.

Later, Carl Gustav Jung (1875-1961), a student of Freud's, abandoned this approach. Jung felt that dreams were much more than mere tools to get to the root of an unconscious problem. He suggested that there was actually much to learn from the form and content of a dream and that the symbols themselves had meaning. He also suggested that there was a level of the unconscious that Freud had overlooked, and this level he called the "collective unconscious."

This "collective unconscious" is also the level from which universal symbols or "archetypes" originate. Jung's theory of archetypes emerged from an experience he had with a patient in an asylum. One day the patient was looking out the window and commented on the fact that the sun was wagging something that looked like a tail, creating the wind in the process. Apparently Jung thought nothing of the unusual comment until years later when he came across the translation of an Egyptian papyrus that told the myth of how the wind was created by the activity of a tail-like protrusion coming from the sun. Since the patient could have had no knowledge of the Egyptian myth, Jung theorized that there must be some symbols that were universal in nature, connecting individuals across time and cultures.

Jung's approach to the nature of consciousness closely parallels that of Edgar Cayce's, although the two men apparently had no knowledge of one another. Cayce's approach came as a result of a dream he had in 1932, while giving a reading to another individual. In the dream, he saw himself as a tiny dot that began to be elevated as if in a whirlwind. As the dot rose, the rings of the whirlwind became larger and larger, each one encompassing a greater space than the one preceding it. There were also spaces between each ring that the sleeping Cayce recognized as the various levels of consciousness development. Essentially, Edgar Cayce's model is an inverted representation of Jung's, with Cayce using the terms conscious, subconscious, and superconscious to describe the various levels of the mind.

Regardless of which model we use, the point is that images often contain mini-stories of events, thoughts, feelings, and experiences that mean much more than simply the image itself. Although these symbols and images can arise from all level of human consciousness, there are essentially only three different types of symbols. There are *archetypes*, which have meaning for individuals across time and cultures; there are symbols that are *cultural* in nature and appropriate for a given nation or society; and there are symbols that are *personal* and specific to an individual.

PERSONAL SYMBOLS
Personal symbols have the most significance to individuals. For example, many individuals have very emotional feelings about their pets. To a pet lover, the image of her or his dog in a dream could be literally associated with the dog or it could be symbolic of the love that the individual feels toward the pet. Conversely, someone else who is allergic to dogs might think of dogs as representative of allergies, as an irritation, or even as a possible health problem. If a person once had a fearful encounter with a dog, then a dog could be associated with something else that person feared. Someone without a dog and no particular feelings one way or another might be culturally predisposed to associate dogs with friendship or faithfulness because of the well-known saying that "a dog is man's best friend." The underlying meaning of a specific symbol is often closely associated with whatever the dreamer equates to that particular image.

Here is another example of a pet in a dream by a woman in her twenties and the dream's corresponding possible meaning:

I dreamed that I was standing in my kitchen petting and holding my kitten. Suddenly, to my surprise, cowboys and Indians started fighting and chasing one another on horseback through the living room. I held on to my kitten and wondered what to do.

The dream suggests that the woman's comfort and security, symbolized by the kitten, is being threatened by some kind of a conflict (cowboys and Indians), occurring perhaps within her own home or work environment (both symbolized by her living room). This conflict causes her concern and leads her to wonder what she is supposed to do about the situation. After providing this insight, the dreamer stated that she was having problems with a new roommate. This conflict was ruining her home life, so much so that she often dreaded going back to her apartment after work. The woman decided that the dream confirmed her belief that she needed to get a new roommate.

Another possibility is suggested for the pet in this dream by a middle-aged women:

> *I am holding a large dog in my arms. One of my hands is clamped over the dog's mouth. I am holding onto the dog, squeezing its mouth shut because I am afraid to let go of the mouth for fear that the dog will bite me.*

This woman seems to be holding on to some kind of anger or aggression (angry dog). She's clutching the dog's mouth shut either because she's afraid of being "bitten" (hurt by something) or because she's worried about words that might be spoken ("biting words"). When I asked the woman about her personal experience with dogs (e.g. "Do you have a dog?") she confessed that she was terrified of dogs because one had once bitten her. I then inquired as to whether or not she was afraid of something being spoken (either toward her from another or *by* her toward someone else) that was angry, aggressive and ultimately hurtful. The woman admitted that she had a "problem with anger" and that she often found herself "biting her tongue" for fear of expressing something that she might regret later. Obviously, the dream portrayed her need to find a better way of expressing her feelings.

Generally, a personal symbol represents whatever the individual most closely associates with that symbol. For example, different places are generally symbolic of whatever an individual associates with that place (e.g. a church = spirituality; a library = learning or knowledge; a post office = communication or a message; the cleaners = that which needs to be cleaned or tasks to be taken care of). In the same manner, rooms in a house can be symbols for what occurs in that room (e.g. the master bedroom = relationships or sexuality; kitchen = home and family or diet; bathroom = that which needs to be eliminated). Cars or homes can represent a person's physical body since both are obviously extensions of one's self.

When a house represents the individual, the roof might indicate thoughts or ideas; the attic, the subconscious or higher self; the basement, the unconscious or repressed emotions, etc. In the same way, the headlights of a car might correspond to sight; the tires to one's foundation or feet; the exhaust to eliminations; the engine to the heart; and the electrical system to one's nervous system. By looking at the thematic content of a dream, an individual can generally deduce whether a house or a car actually represents a physical body or the more frequent symbols of one's life or current situation (house) or one's present experience and direction (car).

In the case of one middle-aged man, his dream of a car suggested he was losing control of his life:

I am driving my car very fast and going down a winding mountain road. The car keeps going faster and faster. I try to apply the brakes but they do not work. I panic when I realize that my brakes are out of control. I try my best to keep the car on the road but I'm losing control. The dream comes to an end when I slam right into a tree.

The literal interpretation suggests that the dreamer needed to have his brakes checked, but the imagery also suggested that his life was out of control. Although he was doing his best to keep everything on track, he needed to learn to slow down and "apply the brakes" to his life. When I suggested that perhaps he had too many things going on in his life and that he would not be able to keep up the pace much longer, he wholeheartedly agreed and decided to begin looking into ways to "slow down."

A house dream by a woman in her sixties suggests that the very foundation of her life had been pulled out from underneath her:

I came home and was shocked to find that my very expensive carpets were being torn out of my house. They were just being ripped up by the carpet people. It appeared as though they were being haphazardly replaced with something cheap that looked much less valuable. I was horrified.

I suggested to the woman that there seemed to be something occurring in her life (at home or possibly at work) in which she felt like "the foundation was being ripped up" from underneath her. From the dream imagery it appeared as though she felt she had no control over the situation and was going to end up with something "much less valuable." Suddenly, the woman began to cry and stated that her husband of thirty-some years had asked for a divorce. She was devastated and understandably concerned for her future. The dream was a reflection of her conscious feelings and worries.

In the following dream by a nineteen-year-old student, the condition of his yard indicated that there was a great deal occurring in his life and that, in spite of his organization skills, he did not yet have everything totally under control:

I was back home in my backyard. I walked around the corner and I was stunned to find weeds at least ten feet high in the yard. I was shocked because I had spent so much time and effort to keep the yard clean. I kept saying, "No! This can't be happening!"

After relating the dream, the student provided his own interpretation. He stated that the dream had occurred after the first day of his anatomy and physiology class. During class he had discovered that they would be required to read twenty pages of "very difficult text" before the next class and that there would be a thirty-point quiz on Friday. The student admitted that the class was much more work than he had first anticipated. I added that the dream seemed to suggest that the dreamer was exactly where he needed to be (his own back yard) and that the task before him was exactly what he needed to be doing.

Other common symbols in dreams include dreaming about other people. When other individuals appear in our dreams, they usually represent something we associate with that individual, or some aspect of our relationship with that individual. Generally we do not dream *for* other people.

If an individual dreamed about the President of the United States, she or he would probably not contact the White House and tell the President, "I had a dream for you." Yet we often say just that to friends when they appear in our dreams. Unless we are very much concerned about another individual we do not dream for them and even if we do, the dream still has a personal meaning for the dreamer. Other people in our dreams generally represent traits, talents, faults, activities, or experiences we associate with that individual.

Here is one example:

I am walking with my brother (who is dead!) arm and arm through a field and a forest. We seem very close and happy, even though I begin to wonder in the dream, "Isn't he dead?" Suddenly, I see my brother's wife and she is dressed like the Virginia Lottery's "Lady Luck" [an advertising symbol for the Virginia lottery]. She waves her hand at us and I start to feel very good about what is going on.

Generally, it is much easier to help someone interpret his or her dream if it is possible to talk with that individual about the imagery portrayed. As stated previously, each person is most intimately aware of her or his own connection to symbols and personal life experiences. In this case, I suggested to the dreamer that whatever she associated with her brother and seemed to be involved in personally (the dream shows her arm in arm with her brother) was about to turn out very lucky, even prosperous.

The dreamer told me that four years earlier her brother had been on the verge of much prosperity in his personal business when he had suddenly and unexpectedly died. After his death, she had taken over her brother's business. She also added that her brother and his wife had been very close and had gotten along well. It became very clear that the dreamer herself was on the verge of much prosperity with the business that was now hers. It was also obvious that the "brother's wife" in the dream was also symbolic of the company business – the "other woman" with whom the brother had had a relationship.

The dream suggested that the business was about to become very lucky and the hopes, dreams, and expectations that the woman had shared with her brother regarding the company's future were all about to manifest.

It seemed clear that much prosperity was about to come into the dreamer's life ("Lady Luck").

People in our dreams can also represent whatever negative traits or qualities we associate with them. Such was the case of a woman in her thirties who had a dream she connected to her grandmother:

> *I dreamt that I was given a birdcage by my grandmother. Although it was a good-size cage, it was much smaller than the bird I seemed to own. The bird was about three feet tall. I wondered what I was supposed to do.*

For a variety of reasons a bird can often symbolize a message or a messenger. Reasons include the fact that a rooster crows to signify the dawn of a new day, the singing of birds is associated with the arrival of Spring, and in scripture Noah sent forth two birds to bring back evidence of whether or not the waters of the Flood had abated. The message to the dreamer seemed to be that she had outgrown something that she associated with her grandmother. For that reason, I asked the woman to tell me what she thought about, or associated with, her grandmother.

Instead of hearing about a grandmother's love or nurturing, the woman told me that the thing she most associated with her grandmother was criticism. For her entire life, her grandmother had been highly critical of her and everything about her: her appearance, her friends, her decisions, her direction in life, her choices – the list went on and on. She volunteered the fact that this criticism had rubbed off on her so that she had struggled for a long time with self-criticism She felt as if she was finally overcoming this problem, which was portrayed in the dream by a cage (imprisoned by criticism) that was too small. In other words, the woman had outgrown her grandmother's and her own perception of herself.

In this next dream, a woman in her fifties has an experience that tries to expand her self-perception:

> *I had a little box of crayons. Someone (I never saw another person in this dream) took the box of crayons away and I was handed a large shoebox full of crayons of every color imaginable. It was larger than the biggest Crayola box that exists and*

there were many more colors than I had ever seen. I heard a
voice tell me that I could sharpen any one of these crayons as
sharp as I wanted to.

Obviously this dream suggests that the woman has many more creative talents (crayons) than she believes she has. The woman said that she had recently bought a top-of-the-line sewing machine with all the "bells and whistles." She also admitted to feeling guilty about the cost of the machine: "Since I don't sew very well, I felt like sewing was something I could never do well enough to justify the expenditure." The woman herself perceived that the dream was telling her that "I have been given many, many talents and I can become as skilled in any of these areas as I desire." She decided the dream was telling her to discard her self-doubts and just "charge ahead."

CULTURAL SYMBOLS

A cultural symbol holds meaning for large segments of a society, a people, a race, a religion, or even a nation. For example, the symbol of a country's flag often represents patriotism (or nationalism) to citizens of that country. A crucifix is a symbol of faith to many Christians; for many Jews the symbol of faith might be a menorah or a mezuzah; and for those of the Islamic faith, Mecca or even a prayer rug could represent their faith. Students of the scriptures may associate a rainbow with a promise or a covenant, whereas others might associate a rainbow with luck or prosperity. In the United States, Friday the 13th, a black cat and walking under a ladder are considered "bad luck." In Egypt, a beetle (or scarab) is symbolic of abundance and good luck. In Ecuador, the dream of a funeral is thought to symbolize an impending marriage. But in the United States the same dream would usually indicate the end of something. In Japan, dreaming about Mount Fuji, the highest mountain in the country, suggests to the dreamer that something magnificent is about to happen.

Certain symbols or icons can represent entire nations. For example, the Statue of Liberty can represent liberty, independence and freedom – qualities that a number of individuals throughout the world may associate with the United States. Many people in the world associate France with good food and wine, romance and passion, and a great place to visit. For this reason, if an individual dreamt about the Eiffel tower, the dream could be associated with a romance, a relationship, or even travel. Because of its phallic shape, the Eiffel tower can also represent some type of a male relationship or energy. The same is true for the Washington Monument. In fact, anything that appears in the shape of a phallus (e.g. a banana, a tall building, a gun, or a hammer) can be symbolic of a man or male energy. Conversely, anything that is more womb-like and receptive (e.g. a cave, a box, a basket or a tunnel) can be symbolic of a woman or female energy.

Dreams that are commonplace and frequently experienced by individuals within a society can be considered cultural in nature. Examples include the dream of falling, which is generally symbolic of not feeling in control of some situation or experience.[2] It can also indicate a loss of personal power and will. The common dream of flying, on the other hand, can symbolize control, euphoria, or an elevated experience of some kind. Other common dreams include appearing naked in public (feeling vulnerable or exposed), or having one's teeth fall out (having things come out of one's mouth that shouldn't, e.g. gossip). The dream of finding one's self back at school and suddenly realizing there is a test one didn't know about, or being in the hallway and completely forgetting one's locker combination both suggest the possibility of feeling unprepared for something that is presently occurring in life. Cultural symbols exist because throughout the world, groups of individuals have often given meaning to specific images and symbols based upon their history and experience, and that meaning has been passed down to people sharing a similar culture and background.

ARCHETYPAL SYMBOLS

Symbols, stories, and images that are universal are called archetypes, the third type of symbol. In addition to having meaning for a large number of people, archetypes can also be seen as encapsulated symbols or prototypes of human behavior and experience. For example, the archetype of the hero is portrayed in stories such as *Superman*, *Hercules*, and *Xena:*

---

[2] An often-repeated "old wives tale" is that if an individual dreams she or he is falling and then hits the ground in the dream, that person would die and that is why the individual wakes up. The truth of the matter is that we often have normal physiological responses while dreaming. Many people have been around a sleeping dog or cat dreaming of running and then watched as the animal's paws move in response. In waking life, a long fall would cause an individual's heart to beat faster with an adrenaline rush, therefore the same thing occurs in the sleep state and the adrenaline and the heartbeat simply cause the individual to awaken from slumber.

Warrior Princess. The archetype of a tragic love affair is told in tales such as *The Tragedy of Romeo and Juliet, West Side Story, Torch Song Trilogy,* and even in the movie *Titanic.* For every possible human condition there is an archetype.

Mythic tales and legends also illustrate archetypes independent of the story's historical validity. Examples include the Creation Myth, which is at the root of all civilizations and societies, as well as the Flood Myth, which is told in a variety of ways in more than two hundred different cultures. Examining the Great Flood Myth more closely, we see that the story is the account of a family that survives a deluge of enormous proportions. Prior to the disaster, the family generally pulls together everything that is part of their world (such as the animals in the story of Noah described in Genesis) and finds refuge in a craft or a ship. Often, the family has no control over their journey as the ship is assaulted by rain from above and rising water from below; they are forced to simply ride out the storm. At the end of the Flood, the craft finds stable ground and the occupants can disembark and begin their lives anew. Everything that was a part of their old world is now a part of their new (e.g. the animals get off the ark as well). The difference is that now all of the ship's occupants find themselves upon higher ground.

Whether or not the story of a Great Flood has any basis in fact, because it is so widespread the tale has an archetypal meaning at a subconscious level. Simply stated, that meaning is one of transformation and change. The ship's occupants underwent a journey over which they had no control and yet somehow ended up in a better place because of their experience. As an archetype the Great Flood Myth symbolizes the pattern of being overwhelmed by personal transformation and change, yet somehow becoming a better person because of it.

What is fascinating about this particular archetype is that in the last decade of the twentieth century the story of Noah had gained in popularity. Almost overnight the market seemed flooded with numerous children's toys, night lights, magnets, collector's plates, ornaments, figurines, and even a television movie – all about Noah's Ark. It is not that this man and his family suddenly fascinated society, but that so many individuals apparently felt in the midst of personal transformation and change themselves that the archetype resurfaced. People felt motivated to put a Noah's Ark magnet on their fridge because subconsciously it resonated with something they were experiencing within themselves.

Another popular mythic archetype is the legend of the Soul's Journey. The story is that the soul was with God in the beginning, then went off on a journey of self-discovery, and will eventually return to the same place it started but with an expanded level of awareness. The Soul's Journey archetype is exemplified by Dorothy's experience in *The Wizard of Oz*, Christian's journey in *Pilgrim's Progress*, Pinocchio's challenges in *The Adventures of Pinocchio*, Bilbo's adventures in *The Hobbit*, and *The Parable of the Prodigal Son* in the book of Luke (Luke 15:11-24). To be sure, no one ever reads *The Wizard of Oz* and exclaims, "That's the best story of the Soul's Journey I've ever read!" but it is a classic because so many individuals relate to the tale's archetypal significance. Whenever a story, a legend, a myth, or a movie can encapsulate an archetype of human behavior, it has the potential to resonate to an enormous audience.

Symbols can also have archetypal significance. For example, the symbol of an old person (or a grandmother or a grandfather) can be an archetype of wisdom and experience because the longer a person has lived, the wiser she or he should be. Another common archetypal symbol is the lion or great cat. Just as the lion is considered "the king of the jungle," it can be associated with personal power or vitality. A very common symbol in dreams is a great body of water. Water is often the symbol for spirit or emotion. The rationale is that water is the source of all life on the earth, just as ultimately spirit is the source of all life. In addition, since much of life is experienced through our emotions, water can be the symbol for spirit or emotions.

The most important thing to keep in mind in interpreting symbols is the individual's feelings, thoughts, and experiences. Symbols are profoundly and deeply personal. If, for example, an individual dreamed of drowning it would be senseless to attempt to impose the archetype for spirit or emotion on that individual's dream if she or he had actually almost drowned in real life. A Catholic's dream about the Vatican could be symbolic of spirituality or religion, but to a Cardinal employed in the Holy See it might simply represent work.

The interpretation of symbols is primarily dependent upon whatever the individual associates with that image or his or her personal experience with it. When these associations differ from the thoughts and feelings of others, the personal association generally takes precedence. Symbols mean whatever an individual most closely connects with them. Sometimes a dream dictionary or another person can be helpful in discerning the possible meaning of symbols, but ultimately it is for the dreamer alone to decide. Therefore, regardless of whether or not a symbol is archetypal, cultural, or personal, ultimately each individual will be the best interpreter of his or her dream images because only that person is fully familiar with his or her current situation, background, relationships, experiences, and thought processes.

Chapter One
Sample Dreams

(See Appendix 1 for possible interpretations.)

A. A woman in her fifties has been extremely busy. The shelties mentioned in the dream had actually been dead for several years when this dream occurred:

> *I dreamed that I was inside my house and all of a sudden I remembered that I hadn't watered or feed my shelties in quite some time. For some reason, I had put them in a shed out back of the house and never went back to check on them. Suddenly, I was in a panic and tried to go and check on them but a neighbor showed up and kept interfering with me trying to go see my dogs. Finally, when the neighbor left I was able to go out to the shed. I was horrified to find that the dogs were gone!*

B. A woman in her forties, who is bothered by all the back stabbing in her office, had the following dream:

> *I was speaking to the office receptionist about the fact that I was being promoted. I had decided that from now on there would be a new dress code that everyone would be wearing. I had on a smart-looking, business-type pantsuit to show her what I was talking about.*

C. This dream is by a middle-aged man who does not get along with his mother:

> *I dreamed that I was speaking to my mother and as I was speaking my two front teeth kept falling out. I'd push them back in but they kept falling out. The funny thing was, I don't think my mother noticed. It made me feel uncomfortable to be around her.*

Interpreting by theme

Stories, fables, movies, plays, and books all attempt to communicate an essential point or an idea to an audience. Whenever a theme can incorporate a pattern of common human experiences or behaviors, the story that communicates that theme has the potential of resonating with the greatest number of people.

Individuals generally learn in English class about the importance of a theme. For example, countless students have discussed *The Bridge of San Luis Rey* (Wilder), which explores how love can be the bridge between the living and the dead. In *Lord of the Flies* (Golding), we are confronted with the horrifying thought that in spite of the dictates and morals imposed by society, human nature left unchecked may not change from its base animal instincts. In *Animal Farm* (Orwell), we are faced with the fact that all too often we cannot help but feel more equal than others, despite our professed belief that "all men are created equal." A theme is essentially the foundation upon which a story takes shape.

When skillfully crafted, a story enables its audience to recognize some essential truth about the human condition or something about themselves. The works of William Shakespeare, for example, have survived and remained popular for hundreds of years because – in addition to his skill as a writer – the themes explored by his plays continue to have modern-day significance. *A Midsummer Night's Dream*, for example, suggests that in matters of love it is often difficult to discern the difference between an outer truth and one's inner fantasy. *The Tragedy of King Lear* explores how individual suffering is most often brought about by our own choices and ignorance. *The Tragedy of Romeo and Juliet* presents the theme of lovers who suffer misfortune and catastrophe because their families ascribe to differing ideologies. This same theme was expressed in the modern-day version of the tale, *West Side Story*. We have all experienced, or at least are familiar with, the kinds of situations portrayed in the works of Shakespeare.

Although themes can be a challenge to discover, with a little thought they can be easily detected. Countless children can describe how *Star Wars* explores the struggle between good and evil. Later, in *The Empire Strikes Back* we can see that one of the most challenging aspects of this conflict is the struggle between an individual and the dark, or shadow, side of him- or herself. Although the theme of the second movie might be more complex, it is still discernible. In plays, movies, books, and fairy tales, the theme is the central idea being expressed as the story enfolds. The same is true when it comes to dreams.

After working with dreams for more than twenty-five years, I am convinced that one of the easiest ways to decipher the meaning of a dream is to first establish a possible theme for the dream's "story." When it comes to dreams, a theme can generally be described in terms of "what is happening to whom" and should be stated in no more than one or two sentences. Examples of themes might be such statements as "Someone is being threatened," "Someone seems to be able to overcome adversity," "Something appears to be easily discoverable," "Someone is running from someone else who appears fierce," and so forth.

Rather than being a waste of time or not worth the effort, discovering a theme can actually save a great deal of time simply because each symbol has a wealth of possible meanings, though not all are appropriate for every dream. By establishing a theme the dreamer can discard those meanings that are not specifically important to her or his dream. The following examples show how finding the theme can be extremely useful in getting to the central of a dream's imagery.

This is the dream of a man in his twenties:

> *I was alone in a sailboat in the ocean. I seemed to be looking out over the horizon when suddenly a large storm started heading directly for my boat. The sky got very dark, the winds started blowing, and enormous waves began striking the boat, threatening to turn it over. The boat got tossed around again*

*and again and I began to panic because the waves were so big.
I was afraid of what came next because I was convinced I was
going to die.*

The water and the waves seemed to be the predominant threat in the dream. As stated previously, water can symbolize spirit or emotion. In addition, water can have metaphorical connotations such as "making one's mouth water" (having desire for) or "being in hot water" (being in trouble). Water can also be symbolic of eliminations ("to make water"). However, the theme in this dream seems to indicate that "Someone is on a turbulent journey" or "Someone is being overwhelmed by something." With this in mind, the most obvious meaning suggested by the dream is not about eliminations, spirit, or desire but the individual's own emotions. Something is going on in the dreamer's life that is overwhelming him emotionally.

The young man stated that he was experiencing much turmoil over his life's direction. Though he wanted to become more involved in theater and the arts, his father (who was apparently very much "the head of the family") had already decided on a business career path for his son. For a long time the young man had known he needed to stand up and speak to his father but he had not been brave enough to do so. The dream was reflecting the dreamer's emotional struggle regarding his own life's journey and his conflict with his father. The conflict was obviously coming to a head and before long the son was going to have to brave the storm and express his own desires for the future.

Individuals often get so caught up in the minute details or the complicated story line being portrayed by their dreams that they try to decipher every element of the story before coming to terms with the meaning. This can be a monumental undertaking and is frequently a waste of time. Over time, trying to go through every image or symbol one at a time and assigning meaning to that symbol might help a dreamer memorize symbols and their meanings but it is not very effective in an overall interpretation. The more an individual focuses upon the details of the dream, the harder it can be to separate from the dream itself and see the story line objectively. Discovering the overall theme of a dream enables the dreamer to bypass unnecessary details and get at the basis of what the images are communicating.

The following dream, by a woman in her forties, provides a straight-forward example:

> *I dreamed that my husband and I were walking and came upon the house of Donald Trump. Everything was gorgeous! Since the doors were opened, I suggested that we walk inside and tour the mansion. Everything about the home was beautiful and exquisite, until we came into the master bedroom. I was shocked to find the room a wreck – everything was out of place, towels on the floor, sheets thrown around, etc. Suddenly, I noticed two dogs fighting in the middle of the room, and all at once one of the dogs squatted and defecated in the bedroom. I didn't know what to think.*

Rather than trying to decipher the meaning of each symbol and then put them all back together, the theme approach discovers the central story line first. Since the beauty and splendor of the house is not maintained within the confines of the bedroom walls, one possibility suggested by the dream might be expressed in one sentence: "Something does not appear as good on the inside as it does on the outside." Having established a central story line, we can now interpret the primary images in the context of that theme.

The involvement of the master bedroom suggests that the woman's marriage or sex life, or both, is in trouble. The two real occupants of the bedroom, the husband and wife, are obviously symbolized by the dogs in the dream. The two dogs are fighting and at least one of them continually drops "crap" in the middle of the relationship. In real life, the woman and her husband had been married for nearly twenty years. To outsiders, the couple appeared to be highly successful and seemed to have everything money could buy. But in private the couple hardly spoke to one another. Often, they did not even sleep in the same room. Their relationship was in chaos. The appearance of the bedroom in the dream accurately portrays the disarray of the couple's marriage. The theme "Something does not appear as good on the inside as it does on the outside" clearly relates to their marriage. The dream suggests that the couple needs to clean up the problem.

Discovering a theme proved extremely helpful in the case of one young woman in her twenties who came to see me because of her depression. She had dropped out of college, was dissatisfied with her life, and did not really feel like she wanted to do much of anything. She had tried counseling but it had not been helpful. She was very unhappy and did not know why.

After hearing her story, I told the young woman that her dreams might provide some subconscious insights into what was really going on in her life. She said that she had never really worked with her dreams and usually did not even remember them. I suggested that she could "incubate a dream" on her problem and afterwards she could bring the dream back to me for help with the interpretation. That night she was to write out the question, "Why am I depressed?" and read the question a couple of times before going to bed. When she awoke the next morning, she would write down her dreams. If she did not remember a dream, she needed to repeat the process until she had a dream that she could bring back for discussion. The woman agreed to try. A dream followed a couple of days later:

> *A friend of mine from elementary school (I don't even know her anymore) walked into the room with an enormous fish bowl that was almost bigger than she was. There wasn't much water in the bowl; it was about two-thirds empty. The water that was there was very dirty and I noticed that the goldfish in the bottom of the bowl appeared very sick. My friend said, "I've been taking care of this for too long, and now it's your turn!"*

Rather than immediately trying to interpret the symbolism, a better approach is to decide what the story is all about. The theme in the young woman's dream seems to be that "Something is being neglected." All the evidence – the bowl is not full, the water is dirty and is in need of being changed, and the fish have not been cared for properly and are sick – points to this theme. We also have the friend's statement that "I've been taking care of this for too long, and now it's your turn," again suggesting that the dreamer is neglecting something in her life. Since she had attempted to incubate a dream on the question, "Why am I depressed?" I felt that if we could only discover what she had been neglecting, we might get to the root cause of her depression.

My experience with dreams told me that this woman was neglecting her spiritual life. Not only do both water and fish represent spirit, but her belief system (symbolized by the fish bowl) was dirty and cloudy. To confirm my impression, I asked the young woman to describe her childhood friend, because very often in a dream the subconscious mind tries to express the same meaning through a variety of symbols. I wanted to see if the friend in the dream could also symbolize this spiritual neglect. When I asked, "What was this person like?" she told me that the girl was very nice, very pretty, and fun to be around. I then probed further, asking the dreamer, "What was different about this friend from all the other friends you had at the time?" Without a moment's hesitation, she replied, "She was the most religious friend I ever had."

When I asked the woman to tell me about her own religious and philosophical beliefs, she said she did not know what she believed. She had not been raised with any particular religion in her family and she did not really know what she believed about God or spirituality. She was not certain if she was an atheist or an agnostic. She just did not know. I advised her that one possibility suggested by the dream was that a part of her desperately wanted answers to such questions as, "Why am I here?" and "What is the purpose of life?" These questions need to be answered to her satisfaction. I encouraged her to investigate different religious beliefs to discover something in which she could truly believe. In this young woman's case, her philosophical and spiritual beliefs had been neglected too long.

This dream also demonstrates how dreams can have different meanings depending upon the experience of the dreamer. If the young woman had instead described her friend as "the best cook I ever knew," the dream might have suggested that her depression was due to a problem with her diet, health, or physical body. In this case, both the friend as a cook and the fish could symbolize food while the dirty water might have indicated a problem with physical elimination.

There is no single right way to state a theme and explain a dream. Instead, when working with dreams, a theme allows an individual to build an interpretation upon the foundation of the central story line. The very same theme might be expressed in a variety of ways, as in the following dream by a man in his forties:

I dreamed that I was looking at my Rolex. Suddenly, I realized
that it was a fake, and that it had been replaced by a cheap

copy. I ran to a police officer to tell him that someone had stolen my watch. However, the police officer told me that I was wrong and that my watch was still there. I looked at my wrist and saw that he was right.

This dream suggest several possible themes: "Something appears to be stolen and is not," "Something valuable has been replaced with something cheap," and "Someone is mistaken about his perception." Regardless of how the theme is stated, however, it appears as though something valuable has been taken from the dreamer. But an authority figure points out that his perception is incorrect. In real life, this man is a well-to-do business professional who happens to own a Rolex watch. He spent many hours working to maintain the success of a business he had helped create. Immediately after recounting his dream, he said that a number of years before he had been robbed of another Rolex watch and had been extremely upset. He had purchased the first Rolex as a symbol of his success in business. The man wondered if he was about to lose his replacement Rolex.

This is a good example of the subconscious mind using a previous experience to bring to the dreamer's awareness a current circumstance that may have a similar impact on the individual as the previous experience. This dream seems to indicate that the businessman was afraid of losing something valuable or was feeling like something valuable had been taken from him.

In the dream, the Rolex could certainly symbolize material success but I felt that a more likely possibility was simply "valuable or quality time." If the Rolex symbolized valuable time, then it suggested to me that in terms of the dreamer's time something valuable had been replaced with something less valuable. Whatever that something was, the dreamer believed it had been stolen from him. However, in the dream the man's higher self (police officer) told him that he still possessed the time and that it had not been stolen from him at all. In fact, that time was still integrally connected to his free will (wrist).

I asked the dreamer if he had a wife and family because, everything considered, it seemed likely that he might be neglecting his family (quality time) because of his focus on work (cheap copy). As it turned out, he did have a wife and children and he admitted that his wife was upset because of the long hours he spent at work. He was afraid that they were growing apart. I suggested that his fear over losing the Rolex was a reflection of his fear regarding the possibility that he might lose his family. The dream also seemed to suggest that he was blaming his work for the fact that he spent so little time with his family, but his own higher self pointed out that this decision was his own. It was still up to him to decide whether or not he would give more valuable time to his family or continue to replace it with his focus on work. The dreamer was stunned by my assessment. After a moment of discussion, however, he seemed open to the possibility that he really did have more control over his time and schedule than he had first believed. He was adamant in stating that he really did not want to lose his family.

The dream illustrates that the more one knows about an individual and his or her background, the easier it is to get to the interpretation of a dream. And it demonstrates that each dreamer is potentially the best interpreter of his or her own dreams.

The following dream by a woman in her fifties resembles a rather common sort of dream, but ultimately the dreamer needed to express precisely how the dream related to her own life.

> *I was going through a building looking for a restroom because I had to go to the bathroom. Every time I came to a restroom, however, the stall or the seat was really dirty (filthy), and I didn't want to go in, in spite of my need to use the bathroom. For that reason, I kept looking for another bathroom, but every time I found one it appeared just as dirty.*

Certainly, many people dreamed about the need to go to the bathroom and have been unable to find a toilet in their dream or have been unable to go once a bathroom was found. Sometimes these individuals have awakened and discovered that they *really* needed to use a bathroom. This type of a dream illustrates how the body's physiological responses can become the substance of dream imagery. It also demonstrates how our conditioning about where it is appropriate to go the bathroom carries over into the dream. Since it is only appropriate to use a *real* bathroom, either the dreamer cannot find a real bathroom or cannot go once a bathroom is found because, again, it is not real. In this example, the woman who had dreamt bathroom dreams before and found that she had to use one upon awakening, concluded that on this occasion this was not the case. She wondered what this particular dream was really about.

To me, the dream suggests the theme that "Someone is trying to eliminate something but has not been able to do so." I asked the woman if there was anything in her life that she wanted to get rid of but had not been able to figure out how. Nothing came to her mind. I suggested that the dirty restrooms might indicate her own sense that whatever she was trying to get rid of was not appropriate and was perhaps even dirty or shameful. This statement still did not clarify for her what the dream was about. Finally, I asked if there was something she was holding inside of herself that she wanted to release and could not figure out how. No, she said. While I was pondering my next line of questioning, the woman finally asked me, "Could it have anything to do with my daughter?"

"Tell me about your daughter," I said.

Apparently her daughter was in her early twenties and had graduated from college. But because she had yet to find the job she really wanted (her mother stated she had been offered several and had turned them down), she had moved back home. Since her return, the mother had experienced one frustration after another. Her daughter was lazy and refused to do anything around the house. She did not do any laundry nor did she offer to cook any meals. When she went out, she often failed to tell her family where she was going or when she would be returning. She often stayed out late and was rude and belligerent to her parents.

Though frustrated by this behavior, the mother wanted to be supportive of her daughter. She felt that her child was going through a challenging, "What's next?" period in life. Many times she had wanted to say something to her daughter about her behavior or her selfishness, but she had not been able to do so. Then the mother added, "I have a problem with conflict…it just doesn't seem spiritual to me."

Suddenly, the meaning of the dream became very clear. The dreamer had been holding onto all of her frustrations and anger regarding her daughter instead of eliminating them in a suitable manner. At one level, she felt that any kind of confrontation would be inappropriate, even "dirty" or "filthy." In the dream her suppressed feelings had become toxic waste products that needed to be released. After discussing this interpretation of the dream, the mother was still hesitant about expressing her thoughts and feelings, but she admitted that there probably was a way she could confront her daughter, helping them both in the process.

Here is another example of using the theme to interpret a dream. In this case, the woman, also in her fifties, expressed her sadness and anxiety over the fact that her life was "spinning out of control." She was very depressed about a short-term relationship that had come to an end. Previously divorced, she admitted that she originally had high hopes and expectations about this new relationship and believed the two of them would eventually marry. Her dream reflected the overall story line:

I am attending a high school play that seems to be some kind of a musical. It is a really good show and I am enjoying myself. After the play some of the actors in the production are on a train, including the lead singer and one of the most prominent couples in the musical. Unfortunately, there is a horrible train wreck. The train smashes into a car that was spinning out of control. To my horror, the lead singer and the couple are killed in the collision.

Several themes can be applied to such a dream, including "Something is in the midst of disaster," "Someone was acting a part in something that did not turn out to be that positive," and "Something that first appeared beautiful, musical, or harmonious led to disaster." The fact that the dream begins in a high school suggests that the entire episode has been a learning experience. Obviously the musical that is "a really good show" is the harmonious relationship that the couple started with and that the woman enjoyed. The train symbolizes the direction in which this new relationship was ultimately headed. The lead singer is a symbol of the dreamer and the prominent couple represents her relationship with her husband. The car spinning out of control is really the woman, totally confused, heartbroken, and devastated by the abrupt end of the relationship. As the relationship ends, a part of her feels as though she has died too.

Though many dreams provide a suggested course of action, this particular dream did not point to a resolution of the woman's situation; it simply illustrated what she had been experiencing. Because dreams contrast and correlate the activities of one's life in order to make sense of them, the subconscious mind often explores the thematic content of a situation in order to understand, clarify, resolve, enhance, or come to terms with that situation or experience.

In this next dream, which again details the use of theme interpretation, a teenage girl's dream provides an objective look at a situation in her life that she had yet to share with any member of her family:

> *I am standing on the sidewalk next to my boyfriend. Suddenly an old woman driving a car pulls up next to us, throws open the passenger door and grabs me into the car. She drives off quickly, leaving my boyfriend behind. I look through the back window and notice that he is running after the car. When I turn back around I see the cutest little bear cub up ahead of us but when I look again it suddenly turns into a ferocious, gigantic bear.*

The possible story lines for this dream include "Someone is leaving someone else behind," "Someone is forcibly taken from something," or "Something that appeared cute and cuddly is actually quite dangerous." In reality all of these themes ended up being applicable to the girl's relationship with her boyfriend.

For about one year the girl had been going out with a boy who did not meet with her family's approval. Her parents had frequently mentioned their disapproval and had repeatedly tried to get her to date other boys. The girl admitted that although she had immediately been drawn to him because "he was so cute," she continued to stay with him more out of habit than desire. She had not told any of her family members that her boyfriend had also begun to display an "explosive temper," and she expressed some concern to me that he might end up hurting her.

Obviously, the old woman in the dream represents the girl's higher self or some authority figure in the family. The fact that the old woman is driving the car suggests that this individual is trying to change the girl's direction. Leaving the boyfriend behind indicates that the relationship is probably going to come to an end. It also suggests that she may have been thinking of ending the relationship herself because she looks out the window at him as the car is driving away. The cute little bear cub that becomes a ferocious beast is obviously the girl's personal experience with her boyfriend's temper. The dream became the final impetus she needed to end the relationship.

One of the best approaches to working with dreams is to find the essential theme that is being portrayed by the story line. That theme might be stated in a variety of ways but it can ultimately be expressed in one sentence or two. This approach enables the interpreter to simplify complex story lines and to bypass a variety of meanings for individual symbols that may not be appropriate for the dream. When discerning that "Something is happening to someone" it is important to remember that the something is generally an activity or a situation with which the dreamer is involved and that someone is most often the dreamer.

Chapter Two
Sample Dreams

(See Appendix 1 for possible interpretations.)

A. An eighteen-year-old girl has this reoccurring dream. She has been try-ing to make changes in her life. About the chewing gum mentioned in the dream she says, "I do occasionally chew gum but only regular size pieces."

> *In the dream I am chewing a really big piece of gum. When I'm ready to take out the gum, it will not come out. In my attempt to remove the gum, it becomes stringy and sticks to my teeth. The gum never comes out!*

B. In real life, the husband of this woman in her forties has asked for a divorce. This is her dream:

> *I was working in a hospital. A man's wife was dying of lung disease. He and his son came to me and asked me to steal some medications for her. They kept telling me how she was suffering. I told them that I of all people understood but I could not steal drugs or bring in herbs that would interfere with her treatment. I also said there was a lot of security and I just couldn't do that. I reached over and got my stuff to leave and I was crying saying that I couldn't help them. I woke up crying.*

C. A woman in her fifties is concern about her friend This is her dream:

> *I dreamed about going into a big house with one of my female friends. To our horror, in walking through the house there were all of these disembodied heads that we had to walk around just to get through to where we were going.*

Interpreting by emotional content

A lthough individuals can have the very same experiences in their lives the feelings about those experiences might be quite different. People usually have very individualized emotional connections to their work, families, acquaintances, and their surroundings. Personal perceptions and feelings are the very things that most often differentiate people from one another.

Yet, in spite of our individual differences, there are also emotional experiences that we have in common as a human family. Most of us can relate to the sadness of losing a loved one, the thrill of an amusement park, the apprehension of starting a new job, the anticipation of the holidays, and the joy of spending time with someone we love. These same emotional feelings can also be evoked by a good movie or a good book. We understand the emotional content when someone tells us that something was a comedy, an adventure, a mystery, a thriller, a drama, a tear-jerker, or a horror story. Truly memorable are those experiences that touch our emotions and elicit some response from deep inside us.

When it comes to dreams, working with the emotional content can be as important as understanding symbolism or discovering a theme. On occasion it can also be the easiest approach to working with a dream because everyone can answer a question such as, "Does it feel like a positive dream? A frustrating dream? A frightening dream? Or an inspiring dream? Just what does it feel like?" The most important thing to remember when interpreting a dream based on emotional content is that whatever the emotion, the dream generally mirrors a situation or experience in the dreamer's life that evokes that same emotion.

With this in mind, a frightening dream should raise the question,

"What is happening in your life right now that is causing fear or apprehension?" A dream in which the individual is being chased might elicit the query, "Are you trying to run away or avoid something?" An uplifting dream might prompt the question, "What are you most excited about, look forward to the most, or makes you happiest?"

If the individual can deduce what activity in life best reflects the emotion portrayed in the dream, discovering what the dream is all about can be a fairly straightforward task. The following dream by a thirty-four-year-old man demonstrates this point:

In the dream I am at some kind of a barbecue with a bunch of people from work. At first everything is fine. Some people are carrying plates, others have a drink in hand. Everyone is standing around and talking and having a good time. All at once I look down and notice that I am totally naked! I am horrified and feel very insecure, afraid that someone is going to notice. No one seems to notice before the dream ends. However, I wake up still feeling very insecure.

Since the outstanding emotion portrayed deals with the dreamer's feeling of insecurity, we might get to the emotional basis of this dream by asking him, "What is going on in your life that makes you feel a little insecure?" Because all the other characters portrayed in the dream are co-workers, a logical assumption is that this dream is about the dreamer's insecurity relating to his job. (Because work is obviously an aspect of life in general, this dream could also be related to something else in life that causes the dreamer's insecurity, but in this case he acknowledged that his feelings had to do with work.)

After hearing the dream, I immediately asked the dreamer about his job. He replied that he was an experienced stockbroker who had just started working for a new brokerage firm. He added that he liked his job and got along well with his coworkers. He admitted, however, that the new firm "did things a little differently than I am used to."

I asked how that made him feel and he replied that he was sometimes worried about making a mistake and he wondered if his co-workers had started to think that he wasn't catching on fast enough.

When I asked, "Since the dream is about insecurity, do you think that part of you is insecure about whether or not the firm thinks you're doing a good job?"

"That's it!" he said.

I pointed out that although he had been naked in the dream, feeling unprepared, insecure, and perhaps even vulnerable in the midst of his new co-workers, no one else had even noticed that he was naked. This suggested that his insecurities were his own and were not necessarily shared by the rest of the company.

A similar dream came to a woman in her twenties who had just started school:

I was standing with the rest of the class and we were all saying the Pledge of Allegiance to the American flag. Everyone else had clothes on except for me. Some people had their shirts off but I had everything off except my underwear. I felt very uncomfortable but there was nothing I could do about it.

The emotion expressed here is one of discomfort. The imagery suggests that the young woman is uncomfortable because she is not feeling as prepared as the rest of her classmates (she is not dressed whereas most of them are). The students reciting the Pledge of Allegiance could correspond to the students' acceptance of the curriculum, or it might suggest their common desires, hopes, and beliefs about the school. It also indicates a shared commitment, as is the flag. The dream suggests that the school is either more challenging than the dreamer believed or that she is afraid that she is not going to be able to do as well as the other students. However, because she has already enrolled and taken the pledge to commit to the curriculum, at some level she is aware that she is going to have to face her insecurities and do the best she can.

Since dreams reflect personal feelings and perceptions, it is often necessary to talk with the dreamer about what is occurring in her or his life. Without such a dialogue, the dream can only be interpreted in terms of generalities. Take for example this falling dream by a man in his thirties:

I am standing on a cliff – it looks like the edge of the Grand Canyon. Suddenly, I slip and began sliding over the edge. I

begin to panic, calling out for help. No help comes, and I con-
tinue to slide. As I began falling over the edge, I awaken, very
much upset.

This dream suggests that panic and fear were a part of this man's life. Probable themes include, "Someone is isolated and afraid," "Someone is in a dangerous situation," and "Someone is falling into a great divide." However, the imagery lends itself to so many possible interpretations that choosing the right one would have been extremely difficult without some sort of interaction with the dreamer.

After hearing the dream, I wondered aloud, "It seems like you're in the midst of some kind of a situation in which you feel like you're totally alone and losing control. Is something going on in your life where you feel like you're losing it?"

"My wife is divorcing me," he replied gravely.

I nodded. Obviously the dream suggests that the man felt a lack of control, as if his life was falling apart. In discussing the imagery I suggested he really needed to find someone to talk to about his feelings: a counselor, a minister, even a friend. Being alone in the situation caused him to feel panic-stricken. In this instance, the Grand Canyon turned out to be a perfect symbol for the enormous divide that had occurred in his marriage.

Let's take another situation, one dealing with a woman in her thirties whose husband has asked for a divorce. The dream evoked a great sadness, as the imagery seemed to deal with the end of her marriage:

I came home after vacation and found a very dehydrated blue
cat. It had thrown up and had the runs on the corner of the liv-
ing room rug. As I put it into a box to take it to the vet, I asked
why didn't someone take care of this. My husband said, "I
cleaned." And my daughters said, "We didn't know, we weren't
here." I was not sure the cat could be saved. The cat had big
sad eyes like the pictures of the moppet kids that were popular
in the sixties and seventies. I was very sad.

Without knowing all the details of the woman's personal life, the meaning of the dream can be interpreted by simply asking the dreamer what was going on in her life that was making her so sad. For the purpose of dialogue, additional questions suggested by the imagery include, "How do you feel about cats?" She loves cats. "What was going on in you life in the sixties and seventies that is now making you so sad?" This is when her relationship with her husband began. "Do you really have daughters?" The couple had two girls. "Is there something going on in your life that they don't really know all about?" The girls were not completely informed about their parent's relationship.

Although it is not really necessary to interpret all the other details once the meaning becomes clear, additional insights include the fact that the woman had been away on vacation. In other words, she had been in a place (or state of mind) where an individual doesn't usually want to deal with problems. The fact that the cat, a symbol of love, is dehydrated suggests that although the woman doesn't want a divorce, the marriage has not really been fulfilling for her emotionally. In all likelihood, this emotional neglect has caused the woman to do things that her husband refuses to deal with (the cat being sick on the carpet). His perception may be that he has more important things to attend to, or he thinks he has already done his part to clean up the problems in their marriage. The cat is blue either because the situation is making the dreamer very depressed ("blue"), or because only her interest in spirituality (associated with the color blue) is keeping her going in this situation, or both.

The daughters said, "We didn't know, we weren't here," perhaps because they are grown and not really a part of the home environment, or because they are not really aware of the extent of their mother's unhappiness. The woman looks for someone to help her with the problem but it doesn't seem salvageable. The whole situation is making the dreamer feel sad-eyed and vulnerable, just like the moppet pictures of the sixties and seventies.

Another case that required a dialogue involves a woman in her sixties. I had to ask her a number of questions before either one of us could determine what her dream was really about:

> There was an old man who was a cannibal. He was running around eating legs off of people. I was very much afraid and didn't want him to get me so I ran to hide in the forest. He saw me and seemed to get very close, but I don't think he ever got to me.

In this dream, fear and anxiety are the predominant emotions. Obvious questions include, "Is there something you're trying to run away from?" and, "Is there someone or something that you're anxiously trying to avoid?" Neither question, however, seemed to be relevant to the dreamer's situation.

Still relying upon the emotion portrayed within the dream, I began working with the predominant symbolism. Since the "bad guy" in the dream is a cannibal who is chasing the dreamer, I asked her, "Is someone (probably a strong male energy) causing you anxiety by trying to interfere with your belief system or direction?" (since both can be associated with the symbol of legs).

The answer was still, "No."

Since a forest is a place where one might become easily lost, hiding in the forest can be associated with trying to avoid a situation, A forest can also represent growth and prosperity, but neither interpretation seemed appropriate to this particular dream. Or a forest can correspond to the metaphor of "not being able to see the forest for the trees" – getting caught up in details, in other words. Only the image of trying to avoid the situation appeared relevant in this case.

When talking with a dreamer, it is often necessary to rephrase something previously stated, to verbalize it in a way that finally strikes a chord. In this instance, I finally said, "It just seems like the dream is suggesting you are trying to avoid something that is causing your direction or personal foundation to be threatened." That statement ultimately led to understanding what the dream was all about.

In real life, the woman had recently signed a contract to buy an old farmhouse located out in the country. After legally agreeing to purchase the property, a follow-up inspection had revealed that the building's foundation was rotten and would need to be completely replaced. Because the costs of replacing the foundation were enormous, the woman desperately wanted to get out of her contract which lacked a conditional waiver pending an inspection. The whole experience was "eating her up" with worry just as replacing the foundation would have eaten her up financially – both interpretations were suggestive of the cannibal. Thankfully, the woman did not have to follow through on the contract. Just as the dream had suggested – "He saw me and seemed to get very close, but I don't think he ever got to me" – she was able to get out of the purchase agreement because the seller had not revealed his knowledge of the property's condition to her.

Since dreams contrast and correlate experiences occurring in the dreamer's waking life, very often insecurities, fears, anxieties, hopes, and expectations all become the substance of dream imagery. Because each of these conditions has corresponding emotions, the emotion portrayed in the dream can become the pathway for enabling the dreamer to take an objective look at some situation in her or his life.

The following dream by a young woman in her twenties seems to highlight some new activity occurring in her life as well as her own insecurities regarding that activity:

> *I was pregnant and now was the time to deliver. I had no contractions or pain. The doctor checked me and left (guess he thought I wasn't ready) but birth had already started. I could not push it out no matter how hard I tried. I was not in a hospital but outside on a chair. Later, after it was born, I was embarrassed because I had asked for two days off to deliver and the baby was a black and white cat. I loved it and we had a special bond but it was still a cat. I was ashamed that I missed work for a cat.*

When the dream occurred, the young woman was two months away from graduation. She had returned to school in order to receive training as a massage therapist. She realized that the "birth" was probably related to graduation or her new career. She thought that the cat was black and white because some part of her was still wondering whether or not her decision to return to school for massage training had been "right or wrong."

Probing further, it became clear why the time to deliver was "now." It suggests that she felt as if the time had come to decide what her life was going to give birth to; in other words, what was she going to do after graduation? The fact that she is having a difficult time with the delivery in the dream suggests that she is having a hard time giving birth to her goals for the future. Her feelings of embarrassment corresponded to her own insecurities about her choice of careers; was it as good (or as potentially successful) as the careers of the other members of her family?

In real life, she loved going to school just as she loved the cat in the dream. School had also given her a number of new ideas (new births) that she really wanted to incorporate into her life. In addition to reflecting the dreamer's thought about her personal future, the dream was also giving her an objective look at herself. In the end, the dreamer realized that her career path was something she loved and the dream encouraged her to look at issues related to her sense of self-esteem.

The following seemingly complicated dream of a sixty-year-old woman can be interpreted either through its emotional content, by its theme, or through its symbolism:

I dreamt that I was standing in my kitchen feeling very much depressed. Suddenly, I started sobbing and crying until it got to the point where I had to blow my nose. I took a Kleenex, blew my nose and noticed that an "N-shaped" nail came out of my nostril. When I looked at it in the Kleenex, I became even sadder. I awoke from the dream feeling very despondent.

The emotion here is one of great sadness. Possible themes suggested by the images include, "Something is making someone very sad," "Something is where it doesn't belong," and "Something is causing pain and suffering." The major symbols include the kitchen (suggesting home and family, or diet), the sadness (associated with whatever is making the woman unhappy), and the woman's nose. Often the nose can be symbolic of the self. It can correspond to the sense of smell, and it is also associated with a number of metaphorical meanings, including: "Getting your nose into someone's business," "Being led by the nose," and "Being nosy." The "N" probably corresponds with whatever the dreamer associates with the letter "N." A nail can indicate that something is being held together, but it can also be a symbol associated with crucifixion – in this case the woman came from a strong Catholic background. The Kleenex is symbolic of sadness or of trying to give comfort to one's suffering. After discussing some of this symbolism and asking the dreamer, "Is anything making you despondent?" and, "Do you know anyone whose name begins with a 'N'?" the woman volunteered the following story:

The dreamer was extremely upset about Nancy, her twenty-year-old daughter (home and family). Apparently the young woman had a serious addiction to cocaine (associated with the nose). That addiction had led to an ongoing need for money to help pay for her habit. In desperation, Nancy had sometimes turned to prostitution in order to finance her habit. Understandably, the dreamer was very disheartened by the whole situation. She had managed to have her daughter taken in by a halfway house on numerous occasions for rehabilitation but invariably Nancy escaped and returned to the streets and the cocaine. As a mother, the situation was "killing" her and she didn't know what to do about it.

Looking back at the dream, the woman is obviously despondent and upset about her daughter's situation. The nail is probably associated with the fact that the mother is crucifying herself by taking responsibility for her adult daughter or, more bluntly, for putting her nose where it does not belong. In reality, Nancy cannot be helped until Nancy wants help. Although still depressed about her daughter's situation, after discussing the fact that she was not ultimately responsible for whether or not Nancy decides to help herself, she felt relieved. She no longer needed to take responsibility for the situation. She could only offer her daughter her love, assistance, and support. But it was up to Nancy to decide when she was ready to accept it.

The following dream is somewhat long and complicated. It belongs to a woman in her forties who experienced nervousness, anxiety, and fear during the course of her dream. But what she recalled most upon awakening was "heart wrenching pain." In real life, the dreamer had two sisters, Aggie and Carol. She was extremely worried about what was occurring in Carol's life at the time of her dream, as well as what she was supposed to do about it in order to help her sister.

I dreamed that I was walking on a large piece of property. My sisters Aggie and Carol were there. I walked over to Aggie and she told me that she had been bitten on her back by a snake. I could see that there were bite marks on her back, but she told me that the snake's teeth had not fully sunk into her. Aggie said she had been bitten over six hours previously and she appeared not to be affected.

As I turned toward Carol, she was talking about another snake that was on the fence next to the property. At first it appeared as a harmless garden snake, but as she moved closer to it I became very nervous. I couldn't warn her in time. The snake lunged out and bit her on the forehead twice. She turned to me, not fully realizing the seriousness of the situation. The bite areas were beginning to swell.

I looked at the snake and it appeared to be wearing a cowboy hat. I was aware that I needed to remain calm and not panic. I asked Carol what doctor she would call if this had happened to her son. She mentioned her pediatrician's name. I looked at the wounds on her forehead again. I couldn't tourniquet the surrounding area or place direct pressure on it as it was a critical area to her head. I gazed at her with love, very saddened to see the wounds, knowing the danger and not sure that it would turn out okay.

I hoped that as Aggie had been okay, Carol would be as well. But I knew that the fangs on Carol's forehead had penetrated deeply. I looked at her and saw her expression – that of a young girl, innocently unaware of the harm. It was heart wrenching. I awoke from the pain as in a nightmare.

The emotional content of this dream suggests that the dreamer was deeply troubled about something related to her sisters (probably Carol), or something associated with herself in relationship to one of her sisters. Paragraph by paragraph, the interpretation and the actual situation starts to take form.

The piece of property suggests a current situation or experience in the dreamer's life. The fact that it is large indicates that it may be a big issue. Being with her sisters can indicate that the dream is about her relationship with them or that it is about something she associates with her sisters. In the dream, Aggie is been bitten on the back by a snake. A snake can be associated with temptation or with energy, but as a phallic symbol it is often associated with male energy. Being bitten on the back indicates that this "bite" has perhaps affected the dreamer's (or Aggie's) support (backbone), or it is something that happened in the past. The fact that the fangs did not sink in deeply suggests that the situation may not be problematic. Aggie's statement that she had been bitten six hours previously led to a dialogue with the dreamer regarding the number six and how it relates to Aggie. The dreamer stated that Aggie had been divorced six years earlier, leading me to believe that the snakebite was the divorce and that Aggie had survived the situation rather well.

In real life the dreamer was not married, and Carol was having serious problems with her husband. Since we learn in the dream that something that once happened to Aggie is now happening to Carol, perhaps Carol is now also considering a divorce. One of the possible themes in this dream is, "Something that happened before is happening again."

In the second paragraph we find Carol discussing the fact that a snake is "on the fence." Being on the fence is a metaphor for being undecided, so one possibility is that Carol, her husband, or both, may be undecided about getting a divorce. Another possibility is that there is a need to keep something out of her personal space or that she is seeking protection from the snake. The imagery suggests that the snake becomes more aggressive as Carol gets closer to the decision or to her own need for protection.

The whole relationship between Carol and her husband causes the dreamer to be very nervous; she can't do enough to warn her sister. The snake biting Carol on the head twice might indicate that Carol had twice given serious thought to a divorce. The dreamer is also worried that Carol is not fully aware of the seriousness of the situation or of her sister's concern for her. The imagery of the forehead swelling may represent the idea that Carol has been thinking (again and again) about her situation with the snake and what she's supposed to do about it.

Since the snake is wearing a cowboy hat in the dream, we know that it symbolizes a man. The hat may also give some indication of the snake's personality. Both Carol and the dreamer need to remain calm in the situation and figure how to best deal with it. Carol needs to decide what to do regarding her husband, and the dreamer needs to decide how she can best support Carol. The mention of the son and the pediatrician suggests a possible reason why Carol has not followed through on her desire for a divorce – there are children involved.

The repeated allusions to danger suggests some kind of physical or emotional harm. The critical nature of the injury probably corresponds to the fact that the marriage may be beyond repair. The dreamer's inability to help the sister's wound represents the fact that Carol needs to decide what is best for herself and how she is going to follow through. The dreamer cannot take responsibility or serve as a decision-maker in this situation. She can only stand ready as a support system. Still, the dreamer is very concerned about whether or not her sister is going to be okay.

The dreamer hopes that just as Aggie has survived her divorce, Carol will be able to survive hers. The dreamer is very worried for her sister and feels badly that there is not really anything she can do about it. The whole issue is an emotional nightmare for the dreamer. In the end, she accepts the fact that she cannot live her sister's life for her and promises to assist Carol however she can, regardless of what happens.

Dream interpretation that uses the emotional content of the dream imagery is easiest when the dreamer can relate his or her feelings in the dream to similar feelings and emotions prompted by a real life situation, experience, or person. Interacting with the dreamer with such questions as "How did the dream feel?" or "How do you feel about that person?" or "What are you feelings about dogs, or automobiles, or forests?" (or whatever symbol is most prominent) often leads to solving the dream. Most often a dream is an encapsulated story that details some situation in the dreamer's life. The emotional content can be the key to peering inside and seeing what the story is really about.

Chapter Three
Sample Dreams

(See Appendix 1 for possible interpretations.)

A. A dreamer in her thirties complains of a relationship with her aggressive mother, a woman prone to critical comment.

> *I was going home and being followed by a Velociraptor dinosaur. I had reached home and the Velociraptor had followed me inside. I raced up the stairs and went into one of the rooms and shut and locked the door. Although the door was shut I knew the dinosaur would be breaking through the door at any moment. Afraid, I climbed out of the window and crawled out onto the roof of the porch that was below the window. I was kind of hanging below the roof so it wouldn't see me. It finally went away but I knew it would be back.*
>
> *Next, my family was packing our belongings: the pets, the food, and the things that we needed quickly so we could leave and be safe from the dinosaur. The dream ended with my being able to watch the car, all packed up and loaded, with all of us inside, driving away.*

B. A middle-aged man recalls a reoccurring dream that he often had as a teenager:

> *The dream is that I am at home in my parent's home where I grew up. All at once I look out the window and am frightened to see that a number of tornadoes are heading right for the property. Although afraid, I suddenly remember that this is something I have been through many times before. The thought comes to me that just as I have survived previously, I'll probably be able to survive this most recent storm. The last thing I remember is being afraid and simply hoping that I will be okay.*

C. A woman in her forties lives far from her family. Her elderly parents are still alive.

I was driving back to Iowa (where we use to visit my grand-parents) with my Dad. We were going back to honor my great-great-grandfather. We finally drove into a dinky town in Iowa and drove up to a large house that looked almost like an office building or a courthouse. A crowd of people, Blacks and Whites, scattered about the lawn just staring. For some reason the scene seemed eerie.

I went into the house and was confronted by an angry lady who seemed to resemble me. She was irate and screamed at me for failing to visit my dying great-great-grandfather. She said that I could not see him any more and then she abruptly escorted me out of the house.

After a little reflection, I was determined to see him anyway because I had come a long way for that very purpose. I went back in the house and insisted on seeing him. Finally, the angry woman relented and led me back into the bedroom.

My great-great-grandfather was so old and aged and frail that I could hardly believe his condition. He was curled up in a fetal position and was as tiny as an infant. As I stood there looking at him in sadness, he opened his eyes as if to speak.

Suddenly, my alarm clock went off and I was awakened. I found myself desperately sad from the feeling of the dream and from my desire to know what he would have said to me.

CHAPTER 4

Metaphorical and literal dreams

Even an individual experienced in the art of dream interpretation can make mistakes trying to decipher the meaning of a dream. Frequently, those mistakes include imposing an interpretation upon the dreamer, relying on associations with one's own personal symbolism and assigning it greater relevance than the dreamer's, or giving a metaphorical dream a literal interpretation.

Imposing an interpretation upon the dreamer occurs whenever the interpreter *insists* upon the dream's meaning regardless of what the dreamer states in response to that interpretation or to the replies that emerge during the course of dialogue. Even when an interpreter is one hundred percent convinced of a dream's meaning, that meaning should never be forced upon the dreamer. In the first place, there is always the possibility – in spite of the interpreter's conviction – that she or he is still wrong. Secondly, a forced interpretation is not likely to be considered by the dreamer or worked with later.

On one occasion, a woman brought her husband's dream to me. Another individual had already interpreted the dream and insisted that it was correct. This prompted the husband to nag his wife into pursuing a medical check-up even though she was, in fact, in good health. In spite of the interpreter's conviction, she felt that the dream had a different meaning. Here is her husband's dream:

> *The dream is reoccurring with some change in detail but the essential story remains the same. My wife is driving her new car. Suddenly, out of nowhere, another car broadsides her and she ends up in very serious condition in the hospital. In*

another version, my wife cannot get the car started because there seems to be something wrong with the engine. A third version has my wife driving down a very steep hill when the brakes go out and it appears as if she is headed over an embankment.

If the dream is literal, there is either a problem with the car and the brakes need to be checked, or "Someone needs to watch her or his driving," or both. However, since their car was new and both husband and wife had a very good driving record, a metaphorical interpretation seems more likely. It was such an interpretation that led another individual to interpret the dream as the husband needing to encourage his wife to watch her health, her stress, and her diet, and to have a physical check-up "as soon as possible."

I can certainly see this possibility. In the dream, the car is hit broadside, suggesting that something is going to come out of nowhere, interfering with the direction of the vehicle (life path or physical body). Not being able to start the engine could be associated with having low energy, having an emotional (feelings) or nervous disorder (electrical system of the car is impinged), or with having some kind of a heart condition (engine). Driving down a hill without the brakes (going too fast in life or having too much stress) can indicate danger unless the driver manages to slow down. All these images led the interpreter to insist that the dreamer have his wife get physical attention before something serious happened. To the husband's credit, he repeatedly told the interpreter that his wife was in good physical health and took excellent care of herself. But the interpreter was adamant: "Your wife needs to see a doctor!"

The wife knew she was in excellent health. She maintained a good diet, exercised regularly, and handled stress by walking, meditating, or "escaping" into a romance novel. She had had her annual physical, mammogram, etc., just six months previously. Though she made an appointment for another check-up at her husband's insistence, she worried that the dream's real meaning was being overlooked.

After hearing the story, I asked her about her husband, his work, and his diet. She said that although she still worked, he was retired and stayed home "tooling about the house" while she was gone. When she was home, she fixed healthy meals, but when she was at work, he always went out for fast food. Since his retirement, he had put on a good twenty pounds.

"Does your husband exercise?" I asked.

"Only in terms of yard work," she replied, "otherwise it's finger exercise on the TV's remote."

"How does your husband handle stress?" I asked.

"By yelling a lot," she said with a smile.

I told her I thought it was her husband who needed to go to the doctor. I suggested that the two of them take another look at the dream and imagine that her image in the dream actually represented his relationship and his hopes for the future. With this in mind, the dream suggested that something unexpected was going to broadside the dreamer's intended direction, that he needed to slow down, and that he needed to have a check-up immediately. The wife agreed with my assessment.

On a number of occasions dreamers have rejected an interpretation I felt confident about and on many of these occasions I would later discover that my initial assessment had been correct. Even in these instances, however, I have tried to leave the dreamer with something to consider. A recent example occurred at a lecture, in which a woman in her forties stood and related her dream to the audience:

I am standing on the ground looking up at an office skyscraper. The building is surrounded by a fence that makes it impossible for me to enter. I notice that the building is very modern and intriguing and I want to go inside, but I don't know how.

If the dream literally had to do with her inability to enter into some kind of office building (work), I thought it might be indicate she was unhappy with her job and trying to do something else related to work. If, on the other hand, the dream was a metaphorical symbol of a phallus (office skyscraper), I felt the dream might be associated with the possibility that her husband had placed some kind of an emotional wall (fence) around himself. I repeatedly offered suggestions that the dream might relate to either her relationship or to her work. But the woman discounted both interpretations. She told the audience that she loved her job and that her husband was very caring. I finally ended our dialogue with the statement, "Well, I guess if I had the dream I might think about whether or not there was something in life that I wanted but for some reason there seemed to be something that stood in the way of my attaining it."

Later, during a break, one of the woman's friends came up to me and told me that although the dreamer liked her job, she was an artist and felt frustrated that she had never really been able to move into art full-time. In addition, on the way to the program, the dreamer had expressed some concern that something appeared to be bothering her husband about his job but he refused to talk about it. As it turned out, the dream might have been dealing with both issues but unfortunately the way I had verbalized my insights did not seem to correlate with the experiences in her life.

Another common mistake made by individuals who interpret a dream is giving their personal symbolism greater relevance than the dreamer's own symbolism. This occurred in the case of a man in his thirties whose friend had helped him with a dream:

> I dreamed that I was under water. The water was great and I was really enjoying myself as I swam through various schools of fish and looked at the beauty of the coral reef. Although I didn't have on an oxygen tank or a mask, I didn't seem to have any problem breathing or seeing in front of me. I woke up really refreshed and energized because of the experience.

In general, a dream of water might be associated with an individual undergoing some kind of a very positive emotional or spiritual experience, since water can be a symbol for either. The dreamer also appears to be enjoying himself and is very appreciative of his surroundings. His friend suggested that something was occurring in the dreamer's life that was related to an uplifting spiritual or emotional experience, but as far as the dreamer was concerned, neither of these possibilities seemed appropriate at the time.

When the dreamer told me about his dream and how his friend's interpretation did not seem quite right, I asked him to tell me what he thought about swimming. He replied, "I love swimming! Although I don't do it much any more, I was on the swim team in school and won a number of trophies. My father used to joke that I was more at home in the water than on land." In this instance, the dreamer personally associated water with his experience and success as a swimmer.

When I asked him, "What's going on in your life right now?" he replied, "I've been offered a new job, and I was wondering if it's the right job for me and whether or not I should take it. It seems attractive but I just don't know." Since the dream had occurred right after the job offer, I suggested he would love the job and feel very much at home in his work surroundings, just as he loves and feels at home in the water. The attractiveness of the underwater surroundings could also be associated with the attractiveness of the job he had been offered. The various fish might be related to the groups of people he would meet in the new company or the various learning experiences (schools of fish) he would have and enjoy. The fact that he did not have oxygen or a mask could indicate that he did not feel totally prepared for the line of work being offered him, but he would have no trouble seeing what he was supposed to be doing. In other words, he would not be a fish out of water.

In my personal experience, the most frequent error made in dream interpretation is attempting to give a metaphorical dream a literal interpretation. Even long-time students of dreamwork frequently make this mistake. Individuals working with their own dreams repeatedly make it as well. One example occurred during a lecture program given by a prominent psychic. Several hundred people were in attendance, including myself, listening to some of the predictions that the psychic had foreseen for the immediate future. One of those predictions detailed a serious earthquake for the Midwest:

> I am sitting at my computer surfing the internet. Suddenly, a map of the country appears before me and I see a tremendous earthquake destroy a portion of the Midwest, near where my wife and I once lived. The destruction was devastating and I began to feel very sad and helpless because of all the people that had been killed or affected by the catastrophe.

As members of the audience began expressing their concern for members of their families who lived in the Midwest, I turned to a friend and said, "I think the dream is about him and his wife; they are in danger of getting divorced." This interpretation was likely because the "world" before him that he had helped to create was destroyed. Certainly, his world could be associated with his marriage, home, and family. The fact that he was sitting before his keyboard suggested that he still maintained some element of control on the situation. However, he simply watched as the place where "my wife and I once lived" was destroyed. In the end, he had some regret and sadness after becoming aware of all the other people (children? family members?) affected by his marriage break-up. As it turned out, within a year of the lecture, the psychic and his wife were divorced.

Perhaps because of our fascination with earth changes and potential global catastrophes, earthquake dreams are commonly misinterpreted. Another example occurred in the case of a middle-aged woman who phoned me with an earthquake dream. She was not looking for an interpretation but for an answer to a question that she had about the Edgar Cayce material. Here is her dream:

There is an earthquake and my house is destroyed. I remember running through what is left of the house, looking for my children and hoping that everyone is still okay. I am in a panic and very upset by the devastation around me.

The woman remembered reading that Edgar Cayce had once discussed "something called safety lands." She was phoning me not for an interpretation of her dream but for a listing of the "safety lands" where she, her husband, and her children could move and not be in danger of earthquakes.

When I began discussing the nature of metaphorical versus literal dreams with her, she seemed irritated. She apparently thought I was stalling to avoid answering her question. Finally, I mentioned that Cayce's only reference to safety lands was brief and elusive, appearing in just *one* of more than 14,000 readings! I told her that my sense was that a safety land was simply a place where individuals were working together with spiritual principles in community and cooperation with one another. I again tried to explain how very often we give a literal interpretation to a metaphorical dream and asked the woman if there were other "unstable" things in her life, perhaps relating to her or her family. But she was not interested in anything beyond a discussion of "lands safe from earthquakes," and the woman abruptly ended our conversation.

To my surprise, approximately six months later the woman called back and told me that I had been right. "Out of the blue my husband asked for a divorce," she said. Somehow her subconscious had known about the instability of her home and family even before she had.

As a result of this experience, whenever someone now tells me about a catastrophic earthquake dream, or a war dream, or a nuclear explosion dream, I try a different tactic. If after discussing the nature of metaphorical and literal dreams I still meet with resistance from the dreamer, I ask the individual, "Do you think your subconscious mind is most concerned about you personally, or about events on the other side of the country/world?" To most people, the answer is obvious.

One of the most publicized examples of a misinterpreted earthquake dream just happens to be one of Edgar Cayce's. Numerous books have even quoted the dream as an ominous prediction of things to come. In the dream, Cayce saw himself being born again in a coastal town in Nebraska in the year 2158 AD. To Cayce's surprise, even though the date was hundreds of years in the future, records of Edgar Cayce's life and work still existed. Repeatedly, this dream has been used to suggest that California, Nevada, Utah, and other areas would simply fall into the ocean one day, because "Cayce had said Nebraska would one day be the Western coastline of the United States."

In fact, Edgar Cayce's dream occurred after an arrest and a court date in Detroit in which he had been charged with "practicing medicine without a license." At the time, Cayce had been depressed and discouraged, thinking about the future of his work and wondering whether or not he was supposed to pursue something else. But a reading given on the dream encouraged him to continue, stating that regardless of what happened in the world – "Though the very heavens fall, though the earth shall be changed" – his work was important and would survive.

Sometimes the literal and metaphorical interpretations of a dream are very similar. For example, seeing yourself eat a salad in a dream might indicate the need for the specific nutrients that could be found in a salad (literal) or it might simply suggest the need to change your personal diet (metaphorical). Dreams of pregnancy or a new birth can suggest a real pregnancy or they might simply be metaphors for a new beginning. Conversely, dreams of death can sometimes be associated with dying but most often they simply indicate a change or a metaphor for the end of something. When both the literal and the metaphorical interpretation of a dream involve the dreamer, either might be correct.

The following dream by a woman in her twenties illustrates this point:

I am sitting at a dinner table with all kinds of meat. There is turkey, hamburger, hot dogs, roast beef, chicken, fish, meat-loaf, and a variety of other meals with meat. Suddenly, I start eating off of all the plates in front of me. I begin stuffing myself on all the different kinds of meat, chewing one mouthful after another without even stopping for a moment.

I heard about this meat dream from someone who had attended one of my conference lecture programs. I had the advantage of seeing the dreamer in person. She was an extremely thin woman with an almost gray complexion. She had dark circles under her eyes and did not appear very healthy or energetic. I considered the dream for a moment, glanced once more at her and asked, "Are you a vegetarian?"

"How did you know?" she asked, gasping with surprise.

The dream literally suggested that the woman was not getting enough protein in her diet, a possibility that was confirmed by her appearance. I told her that the dream was not necessarily telling her to eat meat, only suggesting that she perhaps needed more protein in her diet.

A metaphorical interpretation would have been appropriate if the woman had not had a diet problem. In that case, the imagery might have suggested that she was perhaps gorging on too many choices that she was taking in her life (eating) and needed to take time to savor her experiences or her options rather than simply trying to devour them all at once.

Here is another diet dream, this time by a man in his twenties:

I am in the kitchen standing next to the refrigerator. I open the door and the only thing in there is an enormous container (bigger than a gallon) of milk. I reach in and take the container and pour myself a glass of milk. I think I was in the midst of drinking it when the dream ended.

The most likely interpretation of this milk dream indicates that the dreamer needs more milk or calcium in his diet. In this case, however, the individual, a student in one of my dream classes, assured me that his diet included plenty of milk products and that he often had yogurt for breakfast. Another literal possibility is that the dreamer was eating too many milk products – after all that was the only item in the fridge. But the dreamer appeared healthy and he assured me that his diet was balanced.

After pondering the imagery for a moment I asked the student, "Are you having problems with your mother?"

He looked perplexed and asked, "How does that have anything to do with the dream?" He then added that they had had difficulties and, as a result, had not spoken in several months.

I told him that the refrigerator could symbolize something that was kept cool or chilly. That something in this dream had to do with milk, which because of infancy and early feeding habits, we associate with one's mother. The dream suggested that he kept his relationship with his mother "chilly." The situation bothered him so much that he often thought about it. The dream suggested that he make the first move and give his mother a call. He seemed to resonate with the idea that he was being encouraged to resolve the problem.

Perhaps the most frightening dream that can be misinterpreted is one that seems to indicate someone's death. As stated previously, most often dreams of death deal with some kind of change or transition. Nonetheless, a long-time student of dreams once called me about a dream he had had, asking not about dream interpretation but whether or not it would be okay to call and caution a co-worker about "a warning dream" he had about that individual's driving:

> *I dreamt that Alex – one of the company's spokespeople and representatives – was driving to work and was hit by another car right out front of the corporate headquarters. I got to the accident just in time to see the ambulance arrive. I was very sad because I knew Alex had been killed (or was dying) and I started to cry. Afterwards I woke up and wondered whether or not I should tell Alex to watch his driving.*

After hearing the dream I reminded the dreamer that dreams are most often about one's self. We do not generally dream for other people unless we are emotionally connected to them, seriously concerned about them, or have been asked to dream about them. And even then the dream usually has a personal component in addition to any information concerning that other individual. With this in mind, I suggested that perhaps the dream was metaphorical and relevant to himself, rather than literal and about Alex.

The dreamer had already stated that Alex was a company spokesperson and representative. Therefore, Alex may have represented the dreamer's work. Since Alex's journey comes to an abrupt end in front of the company headquarters, perhaps the dreamer's own personal journey with that company was about to come to an end. That ending may have caused the dreamer some sadness.

With these observations in mind, I asked he if he was thinking of leaving the company. The dreamer was stunned; that was exactly what he had been thinking, and although he had decided it was the right decision, he still had some regrets. All of the information had been drawn from his subconscious and portrayed in the dream's story line. In real life, the dreamer left his position a short time after having had the dream.

In a final example, a young woman in her twenties hoped that the following dream meant she would be getting together with a male associate, someone who was already married:

I am in a grocery store buying things for my wedding. I am excited because I am going to be marrying Ross. While looking at something in the store, I notice that Ross is speaking with a beautiful female cashier and I start to get very jealous. She is prettier than I am and I wonder if Ross might decide to be with her. Finally, I remember he is marrying me and I decide I don't have anything to worry about.

Often, being in a store represents making choices and decisions. In this case the dreamer appeared to have a decision to make. Literally, that decision could be related to her getting together with Ross; metaphorically that decision might be associated with whatever the dreamer associates with Ross. With that in mind, I asked the dreamer to tell me about Ross.

The dreamer had a crush on Ross, whose outstanding feature in her mind was his keen interest in computers and the data processing department of the company where they both worked. For that reason, I asked the dreamer, "Are you thinking about finding a job in the computer field?"

Surprised, the dreamer said that she had recently heard of an opening in the computer department at another company and had wondered about

pursuing the position. She hesitated because she did not feel totally quali-
fied for the position. I suggested that in addition to reflecting her own self-
esteem issues, the beautiful cashier could represent the new job – something with which Ross had some degree of familiarity. The dreamer
needed to set her insecurities aside and pursue the computer job. The
"marriage" she was having was quite possibly the relationship she could
have with her new job.

Essentially, there are two kinds of dreams, literal and metaphorical. A
literal dream deals with some real aspect of what the imagery portrays. A
metaphorical dream symbolizes something else. But it is possible for a
dream to be both literal and metaphorical at the same time. Regardless of
the kind of dream, the subconscious mind of the dreamer is concerned
with the individual having the dream and not with some person or event
totally disconnected from the dreamer's life. With this in mind, most
dreams should be looked at from the perspective of how the imagery can
be applied to the dreamer and what relevance the dream might have to the
dreamer's own life.

Chapter Four
Sample Dreams

(See Appendix 1 for possible interpretations.)

A. A female accountant in her forties dislikes male co-worker, "Bob."

> *I dreamed that I came to the office, and where my desk had once been, there was now a bed. Although I didn't seem surprised about it in the dream, Bob was waiting for me in bed. I smiled at him, took off my clothes and crawled in next to him and we started to kiss. I woke up feeling very confused and alarmed as to why I had done such a thing.*

B. A mother is "very close" to her daughter, Amanda, who is about to attend college out of state.

> *I was in the house and got a phone call that Amanda had been killed. The police were calling to tell me about her death. When I heard the news I screamed and dropped the phone. I ran through the house calling out to my husband, needing him to help me. I was horrified and sick to my stomach.*

C. A woman is frustrated with her husband about their marriage; he is frustrated with his business partner about the company finances. This is the wife's dream.

> *I dreamed that I was standing in the dining room next to my husband, looking at my husband's business partner. I said to the partner that I didn't want anything to do with him because of how he had treated my husband. I no longer wanted to eat with him or be in the same room with him.*

CHAPTER 5

Analyzing dreams through life events

Dreams generally concern themselves with all of the activities, events, concerns, relationships, and thoughts that transpire in the dreamer's life. Just as individuals often communicate with their friends about what is happening to them personally, somehow coming to terms with current events in the process, the subconscious mind provides an examination of the very same information. With this in mind, the ultimate purpose of talking with an individual when interpreting his or her dream is to discover what is happening in that individual's waking life. Essentially, dreams contrast and correlate the events of the day, often providing the dreamer with an objective look at the very things he or she is concerned about – and sometimes more.

The story of Elias Howe and his invention of the sewing machine presents a historical example of how dreams often explore the very same issue that concerns an individual in waking life, while providing additional insights into that situation. Howe had been trying to automate the sewing process. As most people know, when sewing by hand the thread is threaded through an eye at the thick end of the needle. Through years of failed attempts, Howe had finally created a machine in which the thread was threaded through the middle of the shank. Still, his invention was not a success. One night he had a dream. In one version of the story, he dreamt that he was going to be executed by some guards because he had not been able to finish the machine. Rather than being terrified by what was about to transpire, Howe became fascinated by the spears that each one of the guards was holding. In the dream, all of the spears had a hole in the center of the blade near the end of the point. Upon awakening, Howe created a needle with a hole located at the narrow end of the needle, just as he had seen in his dream. The needle now worked and

Howe's machine was a success.

In a straightforward contemporary example, a woman in her sixties also had a dream that provided her with the insight she needed on a creative project:

> *In waking life I had been crocheting a very difficult pattern and could not figure it out for weeks. One night I had a dream that explained the pattern in great detail and I saw myself crocheting the pattern step by step. The next morning I quickly went to my project and put to work the instructions I had received in the dream – they worked perfectly!*

Because individuals do not know how, or sometimes do not wish, to resolve the issues confronting them, dreams can encapsulate one's waking experiences into metaphor and symbol, enabling one to deal with the issue more objectively. This allows the mind of the dreamer to explore the situation in a non-threatening manner. This dream of a fifteen-year-old boy is a case in point:

> *I dreamt that I was barefoot out in the yard. Although I must have walked out there, my feet were stuck in the grass and I couldn't move. I stood there totally stuck and unable to move in any direction. That was it.*

The dream was brought to me by the boy's mother in the hope that it might indicate what was happening in her son's life. According to the mother, her son had lost interest in school and in sports and spent most of his time complaining that he felt tired. The woman thought the boy's lethargy had caused his disinterest in life and she hoped the dream held a clue as to why he had become so "stuck."

It seemed to me that the boy had made himself vulnerable (barefoot) in his current situation (yard) because of something he had been doing. That something had caused him to become lethargic. Although the answer had been right in front of us all the time, it took some talking about her son before it occurred to me what "being stuck in the grass" might be all about.

"Does your son smoke marijuana?" I asked.

The woman lowered her eyes and nodded, "He says he only does it on occasion and it's not a problem." I pointed out to the woman that the boy's own dream seemed to be suggesting otherwise. Apparently the boy had become "stuck" because he had so firmly attached his life and his direction to smoking pot, immobilizing him in the process. Regardless of how infrequent he told his mother he was still doing it, the dream was portraying a very serious problem. I also suggested that since the imagery had come from her son, presenting it back to him might prompt him to give it more credibility than if the counsel regarding the issue had come from someone else.

Dreams can provide individuals with a variety of insights into all the issues that confront them in daily life: relationships, work, health, desires, hopes, and fears. The following dream of a woman in her forties seems to provide precognitive information about a situation at work, where many employees were actually dissatisfied with the way management responded to their concerns. A number of her co-workers were attempting to bring a union into the company to help address their problems. One night the woman had this dream:

> *In my dream, I saw a battle between the North and the South.*
> *The South won.*

In reality, the main corporate headquarters of the woman's company was located in the south and her particular branch was located in the northeast. As the conflict between the employees and the management continued, headquarters decided to close down the branch rather than accept a union and put the rest of their branches at "risk" of being unionized. In a very real sense, the south had won the conflict. (It is also interesting to note that during the Civil War the north had also been associated with the "union," as well.)

In the following case, the dream of a twenty-five-year-old student suggests that part of the current situation in her life was an unresolved relationship that involved her boyfriend:

> *My dream was that my boyfriend and I were talking to each*
> *other. He said to me, "This doesn't mean we are getting*
> *engaged." The next scene we are on a waterbed making out. It*
> *seemed like he didn't want to have sex because he was worried*

about something having to do with the condoms. The scene
changed to me walking into the same room but he was
wrapped up in a sheet waiting for someone else. I walked out
and slammed the door. The scene changed back to us on the
waterbed talking and I was going to tell him I was two months
pregnant but my alarm went off and woke me up.

The dream begins with the dreamer and her boyfriend talking, suggesting that this dream might be about their communication dynamic. The fact that her boyfriend tells her that he is setting boundaries on the relationship indicates he has essentially taken control (or is trying to take control) of how far the relationship proceeds. The waterbed might correspond to the relationship (bed) between the two being extremely emotional (water). Her boyfriend's lack of desire to have sex because of a problem with the condoms seems to symbolize a sexual issue, but more likely it represents the fact that he does not want to "merge" with her in a relationship because of his own fears about being emotionally vulnerable. Why? Because a penis can be associated with male vulnerability and a condom insulates the user from the outside world.

The boyfriend wrapped up in the sheets suggests that he is still wrapped up in some kind of a relationship (bed sheets). As we talked, the dreamer admitted to me that her boyfriend was separated but not yet divorced from his wife. The slamming of the door obviously suggests that the old relationship is still the cause of some kind of contention between the two. The imagery of being two months pregnant and wanting to talk about it has a number of possible associations. In real life, the couple had been dating for two years and the dreamer often wondered where the relationship was headed. Another possibility is that within two months of the dream, the dreamer would have "birthed" her decision about the relationship. Finally, there is always the chance that the dream was precognitive and that the dreamer needed to watch herself and be careful with birth control or else within two months she could find herself pregnant.

Another dream detailing a young woman's current relationship is portrayed in the following example:

I was with my best friend and we were at my grandfather's
house. We were about to eat dinner and had plates piled high

with food. She went outside to look for a place where we could
sit down and eat our meal. When I got outside she had run over
to a neighbor's house to talk. She was showing them her wed-
ding ring. I walked over to the swing to sit down but there were
two dead opossums on it. Instead, I walked over to the glider
but saw a snake skin lying on it. I was going to move it until I
realized that there was a snake next to it. I backed away and
got behind the swing where I sat my plate of food to deter the
snake away from me. He came after me anyway and wrapped
around my legs so I couldn't stand. I fell to the ground and
woke up.

When I questioned the dreamer, she told me she associated her grandfather's house with the ideal place for a loving home and family. Her friend
in the dream was a newlywed and the dreamer expressed her own desire to
get married and raise a family. She admitted to "playing around" in a relationship for the last four-and-a-half years but felt that neither she nor her
boyfriend was truly committed to the relationship long-term. Certainly the
symbols of the swing and the slide could represent their mutual amusement with one another and "playing around." Looking for a place to sit or
to put down her plate both suggest her desire to find out where and with
whom she really belongs. With this in mind, the opossums might literally
represent the woman and her boyfriend, who were simply "hanging out" in
the relationship, aware of its ultimate death but for some reason unwilling,
unable, or too lethargic to do anything about it.

The presence of the snake throughout the dream suggests that one difficulty the dreamer faces in breaking off the relationship is the sexual
chemistry involved. She thinks about setting aside the snake skin (the on-
again-off-again sexual relationship) only to find that the snake is still very
much alive. This is ultimately what prevents her from standing on her own
two feet and leaving the relationship. The dreamer admitted that she often
pretended that her boyfriend would eventually become her future husband
when she knew without a doubt that he would not. She felt that the dream
indicated her determination to finally make a change.

This next dream by a middle-aged woman simply reflects the dreamer's current situation. A successful business professional, she had always
considered herself to be very straightforward, practical, and "down-to-

earth." Recently, a friend had given her some metaphysical and spiritual books that caused her to question some of her long-held assumptions about life. After having read a couple of the books, the woman had a dream that seemed important to her:

> *I dreamed that I saw seven beautiful butterflies fluttering around my briefcase (where I usually keep some documents). I noticed that my briefcase was a different color than in real life. In the dream it was black and white stripes.*

Numbers can have a symbolic meaning in dreams and seven is often associated with issues related to spirituality. Because a caterpillar enters a cocoon and then emerges as a beautiful new creature, a butterfly often symbolizes personal transformation. The dream seems to involve some kind of a personal spiritual transformation occurring in the woman's life.

The briefcase probably represents the dreamer's work, but it is also how she sees herself – in all likelihood she has defined her individuality in terms of her job. Since the briefcase is where the dreamer keeps documents or things she is reading or referring to, the imagery might also suggest that what she has been reading is causing the transformation. This explains why the butterflies are flying around the briefcase. The black and white stripes of the briefcase suggests that the woman approaches everything in terms of being right or wrong, yes or no; straightforward and uncomplicated. The butterflies probably indicate that her old approach to life is undergoing some radical change. However, it could also be that the dreamer is attempting to apply her old right or wrong philosophy to the information she has been reading.

Because dreams can provide additional insights into a situation, they often enable the dreamer to view a situation objectively, to make a decision, or to see the end result of a range of possible choices. The following dream by a man in his forties who had just graduated from massage school provides a good example.

Although he was excited about building up his own massage business, he was also extremely low on money. This shortage of funds had prompted him to look for work. Finally he found a job but suddenly indecision set in. He was unsure about whether or not he should accept the job because he realized it might take up too much of his time, causing him to neglect the massage business that he was trying to develop; on the other hand, he really needed the income. As he went to bed that night, he asked for guidance about what he was supposed to do. That night he had this dream:

> *I am in my living room with my wife and looking out the front window. I notice a little girl out front of our house standing on the lawn. Suddenly, an office supply van drives around the corner and stops abruptly in front of the house. Two men jump out of the van, abduct the little girl, and swiftly drive away. To my horror I realize that she is being kidnapped. I wake up in a panic.*

Upon awakening the man knew that the dream had given him an answer to his query; he decided not to apply for the job but to build up his massage practice instead. Here's why. The dream illustrated his present situation (living room) with wife (family and need for income), trying to make a decision about something (looking out the front window). He felt that little girl on the front lawn was a symbol of his massage business that had not yet reached maturity – it was still a child. The office supply van stopping in front of the house suggested the nine-to-five job he was considering. As a result of the dream, the man decided that if he took the job, his massage business (the little girl) would be taken from him.

By reflecting the image of a dreamer's current situation in story-form, a dream can provide encouragement, even if it is only to continue on the present path. Take for instance, this dream by a forty-three-year-old woman who was feeling overwhelmed by her job. She worked as a webmaster for a large corporation and her assistant had suddenly left the company, leaving the woman with more work than she thought could be accomplished alone. No matter how hard she worked, she could not maintain and update the company's enormous website on her own. Extremely frustrated and defeated, one night she had this dream:

> *I was to perform a musical show with my big boss. I was playing the piano (something I do) and he was to sing. For various, totally ridiculous reasons we could not seem to get our performance started. One time I couldn't find the right page in the*

music book. Another try and the music had turned to text. Another try and the music was for guitar, not piano. Another time I had sat down on the piano stool and it was so low to the ground, I couldn't reach the keys. Another time my boss started singing without me.

No matter what we tried, we couldn't get it together to start the performance. Finally we just looked at each other and started giggling and laughing about the situation. There were several people in the audience waiting for us to start. My boss's wife was there, too. She got so disgusted with us that she got up and walked out. We never did get the show going but we had a lot of fun laughing about the situation. At the end of the dream a little girl about six or seven years old walked up to me. I immediately recognized her as my boss's daughter (who he does not really have). She asked me, "Why did you have to change the passwords again?" which is something I do monthly at my job. That was the end of the dream.

After having the dream, the woman said, "I don't remember my dreams very often…[but] it helped me cope with the work situation very well. When I awoke, I knew the dream was telling me to lighten up at my job. My boss represented my job. The performance we were trying to do represented my job performance. The fact that we couldn't get anything accomplished represented my current situation." In addition, the boss's wife could symbolize the company, and the fact that she leaves suggests that the dreamer's frustration is such that she has thought of quitting her job. The boss's daughter might indicate the dreamer's length of time with the company, and her wondering why things had to change (assistant leaving) when things had been going so well. "The dream was telling me to laugh and go with the flow," she realized, "because I could only do what I could do, and there wasn't any point getting upset about it."

The dream imagery might also include a precognitive aspect. At the time of the dream, the boss's wife was expecting the couple's fourth child. The couple already had three boys. Because of the dream, the dreamer felt that the fourth child would be a daughter: "I remember her as having short, brown curly hair." The child did indeed turn out to be a baby girl, one with brown, curly hair!

Just as in other instances, dreams exploring an individual's current experiences can be easiest to work with by simplifying the imagery down to its essential story line and theme. This approach also enables the dreamer to view the imagery in a detached and more objective way. This was certainly the case in the following dream by a woman in her twenties. Recently married, she feared that the dream was warning them not to have any children. The dream had bothered her a great deal because family had always been very important in her life:

I dreamed that my husband and I had a baby. We got the baby all dressed up to go to a party, even though the baby didn't want to go and cried about it the whole time. On the way in the car, the baby was crying and throwing a little tantrum. When we finally got to the party, the baby just sat in the corner sulking and then started to cry and throw a tantrum again. It was very clear that the baby wanted to leave. Very frustrated and not knowing what else to do, finally my husband and I took the baby home.

Was this dream telling the dreamer not to have children? I was convinced that the dream had nothing to do with having children. Because the couple was recently married, the baby was more likely a symbol of their marriage, perhaps some kind of frustration she experienced as a newlywed. One theme suggested by the story is simply "Someone is being a baby." I thought a likely candidate was the husband, and the dream imagery of going to a party led me to ask, "How does your husband feel about going to family gatherings?"

Her response was immediate, "He hates them!" Though she always enjoyed visiting her family for picnics, on special occasions and over the holidays, her husband had made it very clear that he did not like going to visit her family. "I have to force him to go," she said.

"Do you think he acts like a baby?" I inquired.

Suddenly the dream made sense to her. It had nothing to do with children but with her husband's childish tantrums that arose whenever she wanted him to do something that he did not want to do. I recommended that she discuss her dream and the situation with her husband. It seemed quite clear that he needed to "grow up."

The next case involved a nineteen-year-old girl who was contemplating dating on old boyfriend, someone who had once broken her heart. But she hesitated to go out with him because she was already involved with someone else. During our dialogue process, the young woman revealed that she did not think either young man had treated her very nicely, a fact that became quite obvious in the dream imagery:

I was walking down the street and suddenly two men jumped out and robbed me at gunpoint. They took my wallet, which in the dream I called my "lucky hope" wallet.

Obviously, something valuable is being taken from the young woman. The two men robbing her at gunpoint could symbolize the two young men with whom she has been involved in relationships. The gun could suggest that both men had been aggressive, controlling, or even threatening. Whatever she perceived as valuable – a long-term relationship and eventual marriage, according to the dialogue – was being taken away from her. The dream was advising her not to date her former boyfriend; it may even be suggesting that neither man could provide the relationship she had hoped ("lucky wallet") to find.

Some dreams turn out to be quite practical. The following dream came just as a thirty-seven-year-old man and his wife were building a new home on a three-acre lot in the countryside, near some other custom-built homes. After the final plans for the house had been approved, the man decided to locate the house one-hundred-and-seventy-five feet back from the main road. Those instructions were given to the surveyors and the location of the house was plotted on the lot. That night the man had this dream:

I was walking through our house, which had been fully built. Everything was beautiful, just as my wife and I had imagined. When I came into the kitchen, however, I heard a noise that seemed to be coming from the back of the house. I walked to the back door and was horrified to find that the house was so close to the rear property line that the neighbor's horse was able to put its head over the fence and eat off of our deck! The noise I had heard was the sound of the horse chewing hay.

Upon awakening the next morning, the dreamer drove out to his property and measured where the house had been staked out to the back of the property line. Although the dream had exaggerated the problem, there was no doubt that the house was too close to the back line. So he called the surveyors and had them re-stake the house, moving it more than fifty feet forward.

Although we don't generally dream *for* other people, dreams frequently deal with those we are concerned about. Such is the case in the following dream of a woman in her eighties. The dream had occurred two years previously, but its imagery was still fresh in her mind:

> *I was standing on top of a mountain overlooking everything down below. At the very foot of the mountain was an enormous lake. I looked down at my foot and noticed a beautiful pink rock was sitting on the ground just beneath me. I reached down and picked up the rock and placed it in my pocket because I wanted to keep it. To my horror, the rock fell through my pocket and started rolling down the hill toward the lake. I was totally devastated about losing the rock and I felt as though it was going to be gone forever. However, at the edge of the lake, just before falling into the water, the rock came to a stop.*

Standing at the top of a mountain and looking down below is the equivalent of looking back at one's life journey. But in the process of reflecting back on a successful life, something seemed to still demand the dreamer's attention. Since the color pink can be associated with love, I looked at the dreamer and said, "To me it suggests that something you love (beautiful pink rock) is going to feel like it is going away or you're losing it. It is something you are very emotional about (water). However, even though it is going to appear like you are losing it, it won't really be taken from you."

The woman nodded and stated that a couple of months after having the dream, her sixty-one-year-old son had been diagnosed with terminal cancer. However, more than two years later her son was still alive and was undergoing periodic treatments. The family still hoped that his cancer would go into remission but doctors had yet to change their prognosis. I simply nodded and agreed that her son's condition seemed a likely subject for the dream imagery. In spite of the son's terminal condition, however, he would still out live his mother, because in the dream she had not seen the rock disappear beneath the water.

The following dream illustrates how an individual's struggles can become personified in dream imagery. In such cases, the person attacking or threatening the dreamer is just a metaphor of the real situation or problem. In this example, a teenage boy raised in an extremely conservative and critical household had a dream that seemed to embody his worst fears:

I saw the devil and he smiled and invited me to join with him. To tempt me, he said he would grant me one wish. I decided that my wish would be that all of his power be eliminated. However, as soon as I had the thought he knew it and trapped me in some kind of a glass sphere. He told me that I would never be able to destroy him. In the dream, I wanted to have the same power as the devil but to do good with it instead. Unfortunately, I was trapped in the ball. At the end of the dream, I suggested to the devil that he should try to do good with his powers instead of evil.

It is important to use diplomacy when trying to interpret a dream and relate its possible meaning. After hearing this dream, I thought the boy was feeling threatened by an overpowering and controlling male in his life – the boy's father was a likely candidate. But I didn't think it would be helpful to say this to a young boy who still lived at home. For that reason, my response was guarded: "To me it suggests that you are having some kind of a struggle within yourself about what *you want* to do with your life versus what *others are saying you should* do."

Essentially, the dream suggested that he was feeling trapped or limited in some way (the glass sphere) and that he wanted the power to change things. All he really wanted was to be as powerful as the individual controlling him and to do something good with that power. But the dream could also be a personification of the youth's self-criticism and not necessarily that of a controlling parent. For that reason, I suggested that perhaps the boy was too hard on himself in real life. I told the boy that because it was *his* life, he really did have the power to become whatever he wanted and that it was okay for him to pursue his own dreams. The boy seemed relieved that the devil was not really after him as well as surprised that I knew he felt "trapped" by his present situation in life.

Another dream that illustrates an individual's struggles personified in dream imagery belongs to a woman in her fifties who wanted to become a successful clinical hypnotherapist and was also interested in lecturing and teaching. But she did not seem to be open to listening to the advice of others.

> *The dream began in a large room like a conference hall setting. I was there chatting informally with groups of people. It was the atmosphere of a cocktail party but there were no drinks. I realized that the people had gathered to hear me speak.*
>
> *Instead of speaking from the stage, I chose to walk among them in small groups, teaching and sharing. All of a sudden I heard the large double doors of the conference room open and several men and women entered – they were wearing dark business attire. They looked around, saw me and approached me.*
>
> *At first they were smiling – they handed me a small book. I thanked them and began looking at it. I observed that its colors were black and white. When I looked at it, I felt it was information belonging to some religious sect. I smiled at them and told them, "Thank you for sharing with me but I don't really believe the same." I wanted to return their book.*
>
> *They became angry and looked very evil. They started to chase the people that had come to hear me speak. They were trying to destroy them. They busted the windshield in their cars, stabbed their tires and killed those they could find. But I kept escaping from them.*
>
> *They wanted to stop me from teaching holistic spiritual things. However, I kept going to teach in different areas and the same thing kept happening. The people in the business suits were always looking for me and would always try to destroy the people that came to listen to me.*
>
> *My students asked if I was afraid they would kill me and I said, "No. Don't be afraid. They can only kill you but they can't*

destroy your soul." I said, "I am not afraid of dying or of them torturing me. I am only concerned that they keep me from being able to teach and share the truth. That is why I keep running and moving so I can teach and share as much as I can before they find out where I am."

The dream lends itself to a wide variety of interpretations. From the very first it appears as though the dreamer is very comfortable (or would like to become comfortable) speaking in an informal manner with her audiences and/or clients. She also feels as though she has something to say because people seem willing to listen to her speak. Her desire to be informal is also apparent in her refusal to use the stage, preferring instead to "walk among" her participants.

The people who interrupt her gathering are dressed in dark business attire. By giving her their black and white ("right or wrong;" "appropriate or inappropriate;" "yes or no") booklet, they share their beliefs, which the woman rejects. This suggests that someone or something is critical of her, or how she is doing her job. Another possibility is that the informal approach she prefers is being threatened by more professional, "by the book" standards demanded by contemporary society. The dream could also pertain to legal issues, insurance, licensing, professionalism, and even marketing requirements. In talking with the dreamer it became clear that these issues were very foreign to the "real work" that interested her.

In the middle of the dream we learn that intruders are "trying to destroy" what she hopes to accomplish. Breaking windshields could be symbolic of destroying someone's "vision," or goal, just as slashing tires can represent trying to impede someone's progress. It is also possible that the woman was involved in personal sabotage as a means of escaping her responsibilities.

Essentially, the intruders threaten to prevent the dreamer from teaching things of a spiritual nature. No matter where she goes, there they are. Because of this dynamic, it is logical to ask the dreamer if she found her career pursuits challenging. To this query, she responded that it had been "very challenging" but that she felt driven to continue her efforts. In the end, the dreamer has put to rest her fears by talking with her students. We learn that she really had nothing to be afraid of; she cannot really be killed. She will continue her work.

I pointed out to the dreamer that her fears of doing things differently would not destroy what she hoped to convey to her clients. I recommended that she stop running away from doing things differently than she had first imagined, whether it meant being more professional or more traditional. As it turned out, others had also recommended doing things more "by the book" but she had yet to heed their advice.

The next case involves a young woman nervously considering her future and her career. Family members believed she was not old enough to make mature decisions. The young woman was struggling with this doubt and her own feelings about what she felt was right. Finally, the following dream set her fears to rest and told her that she really was headed in the right direction after all:

> *I dreamt that I had a beautiful baby boy. He had the brightest blue eyes and was very young. I felt so close to my baby. I could feel a very intense love for him in the dream. Bridget (one of my classmates) lived across the street from me. She was babysitting for me and when I came to pick my baby up, she wouldn't give him to me. Everyone seemed to think that I couldn't take care of him. However, I knew I could and they didn't know how deeply I loved him. I looked everywhere for my baby because some other people (I don't recognize them but in the dream I knew them) had taken him. I finally found him at a park in a clubhouse with these people. I got him back from them and I was so happy. The two of us got into my car. It was a little red Omni and we drove away. I had the car all packed up because I knew I had to go where no one would try to take him again.*

To the dreamer, Bridget symbolizes someone who always seemed confident, capable, and decisive about what she wanted to do, all qualities the dreamer was trying to emulate in her own life. The baby represents a new beginning full of potential. The baby's blue eyes suggest that the dreamer was discovering something about her own personal spirituality in the process of pursuing her dreams.

"I think the fact that I love my baby so much in the dream symbolizes the love of what I want to do," the young woman said. "However, people trying to take the baby away from me represents my own fear of failure and not being able to hold on to this beginning. In the end of the dream, getting my baby back and driving away means that I will be able to hold on." In addition, I felt that the red car in the dream represented the dreamer's energy and the determination to succeed, though it might not be what family members had in mind for her.

The importance of diplomatically exploring the possible meaning of a dream became evident when a friend who works with dream interpretation brought me a dream that had been sent to her for evaluation. After reading the dream, which seemed to be that of a middle-aged woman, I turned to my friend and said, "Well, it seems that the woman's husband is either having an affair or thinking about having an affair." My friend nodded, for that had also been her interpretation:

I am standing on the front porch of a beautiful Victorian home, which is not my home in real life but seemed to be my home in the dream. Everything is beautiful! The home is covered with ornate gingerbread trim. The porch has a couple of rockers and looks out over a gorgeous manicured lawn. Everything is in its place. The yard is surrounded by a quaint white picket fence. Even though I am not aware of where my husband is, I seem very happy.

I find myself thinking about how wonderful my surroundings are when I suddenly notice that a male deer is out on the edge of the yard all by itself. For some reason the deer seems very sad. Although it is in my yard, it stands next to the fence and seems to want to get out. It hangs its head and antlers over the fence and watches with wide-eyed attention as three female doe run by the yard just on the other side of my fence.

The dream suggests that the woman's ideal of having everything in her life perfect is not realistic. At the very least, her sense of life and her relationship is not being shared by her male counterpart (the deer trying to get out of the yard). This is also represented by the woman's lack of awareness of her husband in the dream. Her husband seems discontent and even sad about his situation. As a result he may be looking for new relationship opportunities (three female doe).

I realized that it would not be wise to tell the woman, "Your husband is thinking about having an affair." Perhaps the woman's dream only portrayed her husband dissatisfaction with his life and not a real affair. Besides, the subconscious mind only relates information to individuals in ways they can assimilate it, so people working with dream interpretation need to do likewise. For that reason, I encouraged the dreamer to begin communicating with her husband more fully about their life together because the dream suggested that "Your idealized view of your life and your surroundings is not necessarily being shared by your husband. The two of you need to talk about it."

Because it was not possible to ask the dreamer about her dream, coming to a clear understanding of why three doe are present in the dream rather than one is speculative at best. But the number three could indicate how long their marriage had lasted, the number of years her husband has been dissatisfied, the number of his prior relationships, or the fact that he is looking at several different opportunities.

In our final dream, we explore the current situation of a woman in her twenties who had gone to Jamaica with a girlfriend, leaving her boyfriend at home. Her dream occurred halfway through their vacation:

> *I was in an underground cave that went on for miles and miles. While under the earth I came upon all of these trolls. The trolls were very happy to see me because the cave was filled with beautiful crystals that could only be energized by a human being and they wanted me to energize them. After I did, they gave me some stakes that they wanted hammered into the ground. I followed their instructions. Later, I was taken even deeper into the cave (below where we had been), and I was horrified to find that the stakes had gone through to a lower cave and impaled a man to death. I used the power of the crystals to destroy all of the trolls because of what they had made me do.*

The underground cave can represent the subconscious, or it might correspond to an individual's "lower self" or sexual desires. A cave can also symbolize the womb and female sexuality. In talking with the dreamer, she admitted that one outstanding feature of her vacation had been the "very good-looking" Jamaican males "hitting on" her. She admitted that she had been tempted to have an affair but decided against it because she really loved her boyfriend. This entire situation was portrayed in her dream.

Trolls can be a symbol of something that diverts someone from his or her path. Because they are often portrayed in the literature as interested in stealing children, trolls can also be symbolic of something that steals innocence. Therefore, the trolls represent the men hitting on the dreamer and trying to take her "innocence." Crystals are associated with dreams or desires. But in the dream, these crystals can only be energized by a human being. The only thing that sets a human apart from the rest of Creation is free will. Therefore, the crystals in this case seem to symbolize the dreamer's own free will.

The dream imagery suggests that the dreamer can use her free will to hammer (a reference to a phallic image?) stakes into the ground. But that will only lower herself even deeper into her sexual feelings, resulting in the destruction of her relationship with her boyfriend (impaled a man to death). In the end, the dream shows the woman using her free will to destroy the trolls, suggesting that she has rebuked their advances.

Because dreams contrast and correlate the events of the day, they serve primarily as a means for the dreamer to wrestle with the issues, concerns, and feelings that have been on the individual's conscious mind. Dreams can provide an objective look at known facts, explore new insights, and even offer potential solutions. This allows individuals to come to terms with current events, make sense of their lives, or discover solutions to problems that they have been facing. By evaluating current life events, dreamers can address their physical, mental, or spiritual well-being. This process is ongoing and assists individuals even if they do not consciously work with their dreams. At the very least, this process of examining one's life is extremely helpful to the subconscious mind. Of course, the process becomes even more beneficial once individuals begin to consciously examine what their dreams are trying to tell them.

Chapter Five
Sample Dreams

See Appendix 1 for possible interpretations

A. A woman in her fifties is in the midst of life changes and needs to make decisions about her future.

> *I dreamt that there was an elegant looking woman who was standing by herself. She appeared calm and collected. Suddenly I noticed that she was missing her entire right arm. There wasn't even a stub where her arm should have been. I was carrying a white shawl at the time and I took it over to the woman and draped it around her shoulders. I don't know if I was trying to cover her missing arm or help her stay warm. She seemed appreciative and thanked me.*

B. A twenty-year-old man has moved to a university town to attend school. He has not yet found a job and is worried.

> *I am trying to take a picture of an awesome sunset down a road. It gets better and better. The sky gets very cloudy with bright orange colors. As I try to take the picture, a little boy gets in the way. I keep hoping he will move but when he does the sunset is gone.*

C. A nineteen-year-old woman has developed romantic feelings for a male friend, Patrick, and is worried that the feelings will affect their friendship.

> *I had a dream that I was at a party. It seemed to be my house but it wasn't. I was outside and saw a snake in our neighbor's yard that looked like an anaconda. I went back in the house, found my friend Patrick, and told him about the snake. When we went outside to look for it, it wasn't there. Afterwards, we walked through another room leading outside to the front yard because he had to leave. On the way to Patrick's car, we*

passed some friends playing cards. Before he left, he kissed me on the cheek, then we hugged and he kissed me on the lips.

The next thing I remember was being at another house with another guy who is a friend. We are sitting on some monkey bars. Then I saw the snake again. This time it was winding itself around the pole and looping itself through the bars. I was scared but my friend told me it would be all right and wouldn't hurt me. Then Patrick came out (the other friend seemed to be gone) and we watched the snake go to the other yard.

Dreams for the body, mind, and soul

Years ago, medicine simply addressed the physical needs of the body. But since each individual is obviously much more than a physical organism, holistic medicine today addresses an individual's mental and spiritual needs as well. With this idea in mind, it is worth noting that dreams also explore every area of an individual's life – the physical, the mental, and the spiritual. Whether the issue concerns an individual's health, emotions, hopes, aspirations, or spiritual values and beliefs, dreams can explore whatever the dreamer faces in waking life. Dreams that reflect current life events come in three categories: dreams that relate to the body, dreams that provide psychological insights into life's events, and dreams that nurture the soul.

We saw earlier how dreams can provide dietary recommendations and suggestions. But dreams for the body are not limited to diet alone. Take this example from the life of psychic Edgar Cayce. While suffering from a miserable cough and cold, Cayce had a dream. In it he saw himself in the kitchen mixing a concoction of boiling water, honey, glycerin, simple syrup, horehound, benzoin, and whiskey. Upon awakening, he realized that the formula appeared to be a cough syrup made up of harmless ingredients. After preparing and taking the formula, he finally found relief from his cough.

Here is another example from the Cayce files. One night a woman had a dream in which her mother (who was still alive) appeared to her, saying "You should go to the osteopath. You ought to be ashamed of yourself! If your husband wants you to go to the osteopath, you should go!" Cayce's interpretation of the dream was twofold: to assure the woman that valid information could come to her through the dream state and to affirm that *she needed to see an osteopath!*

A similar situation occurred in the following dream from the 1970s. In this case, a man in his forties had developed chest pains and had gone to see a doctor about his condition. The doctor consulted specialists who wanted to perform a coronary bypass immediately, even though the man followed a nutritious diet and had a good family history that did not indicate a predisposition to heart problems. Since the man felt that his chest pains were probably stress-related, he declined the operation. That night he had this dream:

> *My dream was that a Model A Ford was sitting by the side of the road with its hood up. Two mechanics were working on the engine. I realized that the two mechanics looked like the two doctors I had seen the previous day, only in the dream they were wearing big, baggy pants like circus clowns.*

In working with his dream, the man realized that he was the car, as the car dated back to his birth in 1929. He thought that the mechanics working on the engine corresponded to the doctors who had examined his heart. In spite of their diagnosis and their insistence on surgery, the dream essentially showed him that the two had been "clowns," and their diagnosis, inappropriate for the occasion. Because of the dream, the man remained firm in his decision to forgo surgery. Instead, he focused on reducing his stress. More than twenty years later, the dreamer was still doing fine and never regretted his decision.

In another example, a nineteen-year-old man had gone to a college in the Rocky Mountains. It was the middle of the winter and the dormitory always seemed cold. During a phone conversation with his grandmother, the young man complained about never feeling warm at night. To his surprise, a week later his grandmother mailed him an electric blanket, which he began using immediately. Because he had been so cold, he left the blanket plugged in all night, causing him to feel warm "for the first time since coming to school."

Sometime later, the young man found himself feeling tired and very lethargic each morning upon awakening. He thought that his condition must somehow be related to "Rocky Mountain weather." One night he had this dream:

I saw myself standing in the bathroom in my grandmother's house, looking in the mirror. I had my electric blanket draped over my shoulders and around my body. Suddenly, I opened up the blanket and stared in the mirror. I was horrified to see that my body was covered with hundreds of leeches.

The dream led the young man to think that the blanket was actually draining his energy. It was the blanket that made him feel tired each morning, not the weather. From that day on he plugged in the blanket about a half-hour before going to bed and unplugged it just before getting under the covers. After following through on this dream message, he no longer felt exhausted each morning when he got up.

A sports injury from high school seemed to be the cause, thirty years later, of the following dream by a businessman in his forties. The man, who had injured his hip playing football, thought nothing more of the problem until three decades later when he began having alternate "numb and throbbing" pains near the site of the injury. This dream provided the prognosis:

A female surgeon is in a hospital room examining me. After examining me, she looks up, touches the area of my hip and says, "There's no longer any doubt, this has got to come out."

The dream prompted the businessman to make an appointment with his doctor, who referred him to a surgeon. After examining the hip, the surgeon recommended and later performed surgery to remove old scar tissue caused by internal bleeding decades previously. After the surgery and his recovery, the dreamer was no longer bothered by the pain in his hip.

A much more complicated dream so scared the wife of a man in his sixties named Bob that she changed the course her husband's treatment. In real life, a lung problem had caused his early retirement. Apart from the lung condition, Bob was healthy until he contracted pneumonia. Because of the pneumonia he was treated with antibiotics and had to briefly use oxygen. Although he was sent home from the hospital, he never fully recovered and was hospitalized a short time later for pneumonia again. And again he was put on oxygen. Bob was treated and released four days later but was readmitted to the emergency room a few hours later because of breathing problems.

Again he was treated and new tests were performed before releasing him to go home, still on oxygen. Within two weeks the hospital called and informed the couple that the tests indicated that Bob had contracted tuberculosis. Though medication was begun immediately, Bob's condition deteriorated. A short time later he was back in the emergency room.

Further tests indicated that Bob's problem wasn't tuberculosis after all but a strain of drug-resistant pneumonia. For insurance reasons, Bob had to transfer to another hospital, but because the new hospital only recognized the tuberculosis diagnosis, they continued with the treatment for tuberculosis. Bob's condition deteriorated even further while they waited for the "official" diagnosis specifying the strain of pneumonia. For days he had to work at every breath. Finally, they gave him the antibiotics he needed and Bob recovered well enough so that they could send him home, still on oxygen.

By this time, he was using four or five liters of oxygen a minute and was hooked to a fifty-foot lead, spending most of his time in a recliner. However, in spite of the various treatments he was still not well. Finally, the following dream scared Bob's wife into finding a different course of action:

I dreamed that Bob had awakened and his condition has worsened. We hurried to the doctor's to see if we could get him some help. Bob was driving to the doctor's and on the way he missed the turn. I told him he had missed it and he would have to turn around and go back. He kept driving and I was really irritated that he didn't turn around. Finally, after twenty blocks he turned around and went back.

When we entered the clinic, we separated so that each of us could try and find some help. I talked to the nurses at the desk and told them that Bob was worse and needed to see the doctor. They said they would squeeze him in. Bob returned and said that he hadn't been able to get an appointment and I told him not to worry, that the nurses said they would take care of it. I pointed them out to him and they said that they would take

*care of Bob first since he was on oxygen. I realized that I
should go out to the car and get an extra oxygen tank in case
he ran out. I left Bob and went out to the parking lot to get a
tank out of the car. I had difficulty locating the car and I
noticed two men in the parking lot. They seemed to be just
ordinary men, decently dressed. I became afraid that the car
couldn't be found but then I realized, "Oh, well, this is a hospital and they will certainly have oxygen."*

    *I went back in the building and saw Bob in the hallway. He
had collapsed and was flopping around the floor with uncontrollable movements. I went up to the nurses and asked what
had happened. They said he was having difficulty breathing.
The two men I had seen in the parking lot approached, said
they were doctors and that they would take care of him. They
got an assist chair with handles on either side to help carry
him.*

    *When they finally came by carrying Bob, he looked like he
was sitting Indian fashion. He said that his legs hurt and as I
looked closer I was shocked to find that his legs had been cut
off. I was very upset and asked how they had done it and they
said, "We did it with drugs." I was angry, "Can you do that
without our permission?" I asked to see the doctor who had
done it and they said he had already left. They offered to get a
public relations doctor to smooth things over and then the
dream ended.*

Fearing that the continued course of treatment would further erode her
husband's health, the woman related her dream to her husband. She told
him, "It's true, they have cut off your legs. You are immobilized and
chained to the oxygen. The doctors are treating you with drugs but you
need more." As a result, the couple pursued a more holistic approach and
decided to admit him to a clinic that specialized in complimentary medicine. "That experience led my husband being taken off the oxygen and a
complete healing," she relates. In retrospect, the woman realized that the
twenty blocks portrayed in the dream were symbolic of the twenty weeks it
had taken to turn Bob's illness around.

    In addition to dreams that correspond to the body's physical condition, dreams can also provide psychological insights into life events. Such dreams can provide the dreamer with an examination of feelings, worries, thoughts, and desires, as well as greater self-understanding and even emotional healing.

The following dream from the Edgar Cayce files occurred while Cayce had been extremely worried about his personal finances. He was very concerned about being able to support his family. One night he had a dream in which he found himself walking along a street in Paris with the Duke and Duchess of Windsor and Jesus. They came to a sidewalk café and Cayce invited his three companions to join him in a glass of champagne. The four travelers sat down and had a pleasant conversation. When the time came to leave and the Duke and Duchess got up, Cayce and Jesus were left alone at the table. To Cayce's horror, he realized that although he had invited everyone for drinks, he only had a few pennies in his pocket and would not be able to pay. When he pulled the change out of his pocket, Jesus simply laughed and said, "Will I have to send you after a fish too?"

Because dream imagery can utilize personal symbols familiar to the dreamer, Cayce was very much aware of the reference to fish. In the book of Matthew, the Apostles are traveling to Capernaum and need money to pay the tax of admittance to the city. Since they had no money, Jesus sent them to catch a fish. The first fish caught had a coin in its mouth – the very amount needed to pay the tax. With this in mind, the dream was encouraging Cayce to have faith and to realize that whatever he needed to support his family would be provided.

In this second example, a couple is facing marital discord. During this time, the husband brought a dream to Cayce for interpretation. In the dream, he saw himself riding on a train, his wife sitting next to him. As he watched the passage of scenery out the window, he noticed his wife trying to measure the window with a croquet mallet. The husband scolded her and exclaimed, "It can't be measured that way!"

Cayce interpreted the dream as an exploration of the different approaches the couple had taken trying to measure the success of their relationship. Whereas the husband seemed content to measure success by how much material progress they made in their journey together, the wife was much more interested in measuring how much fun they were having. Apparently the couple needed to communicate about what it was they were trying to achieve in life together.

In a contemporary example, a young woman's worries and feelings of financial inequality are portrayed in a dream that occurred while she was at college studying for her Ph.D.:

> *I was on the main road in my hometown, where I am not currently living. On the road next to me were cars. It seemed that my body was my car and that everyone else had a real car. I was crawling around on the road with my blankets around me trying to keep up with the actual cars. I was extremely afraid and woke up just as I was trying to make a left turn into a mall.*

At the time of the dream, the young woman was financially strapped and felt economically inferior to other people. Because of her lack of finances and her need to focus her time and energy into her schoolwork, her life seemed to lack any personal security or comfort. The dream imagery indicated to her that she was overly concerned about material issues (turning in to the mall) or that she might have made a wrong career choice. In time, she finished her Ph.D. and her finances improved, but she never did choose to become a professor, which had been her career goal at the time of the dream.

The following dream by a middle-aged woman is one that reoccurred every year around Christmas, and reflected her worst fears about not being prepared for the holidays. The dream really bothered her because in spite of her hectic life and schedule, she really tried to make Christmas an enjoyable experience for every member of her family.

> *Every year around Christmas I dream that it is Christmas day and I am with my family to celebrate. When it's time for gift giving, I realize with horror that I have forgotten to buy any gifts for anyone. I scramble around trying to pull together anything to give to my family. I am so embarrassed and ashamed but my family doesn't seem to care.*

Obviously, the dream portrays the woman's fears about not being prepared for Christmas because of her busy schedule. But at the same time the dream provides some reassurance, that regardless of how much or how little she is able to accomplish, her family would still enjoy the holidays. In other words, she needed to stop worrying so much, do what she could without putting so much pressure on herself, and simply enjoy the season.

The next dream is by a man in his fifties who prided himself on his ability to serve as a peacemaker in family issues. But one of his children was no longer responsive to the rational and straightforward discussions that had worked so well with the rest of his family. One night he had a dream that encouraged him to change his approach:

My car is broken down. I notice it is a Nash Ambassador, like the one I used to own years ago. Unfortunately, there is nothing I can do to make the car work.

Upon awakening, the man felt that the dream was telling him that his diplomatic approach (the ambassador) would not work in some emotional situations. Because of the dream, the man felt it was appropriate to adopt a more assertive approach. The approach succeeded and the situation with his child was resolved.

Another dream exploring psychological issues involves a women in her fifties experiencing marital difficulties. She was torn between leaving the situation or trying to make it work. Sometimes she felt that it was her responsibility to try and fix the problem, on other occasions she felt trapped by the situation and desperately wanted a way out. "I needed my own space," explained the woman, "because I was feeling like a prisoner in my own home." One day she finally decided to move out. But that night she began having second thoughts and as she drifted off to sleep she thought to herself, "Perhaps I should try and save this marriage one more time." This dream followed:

I dreamt that I was trying to go back into a building that was being destroyed. I was trying to save something. Everything around me was crumbling and I suddenly realized that there was nothing in the building worth saving. Saving my life was more important.

The next morning the woman knew instantly what the dream meant. She was in danger of destroying herself by remaining in the situation; it could not be saved because there was nothing worth saving. The dream became the final impetus the woman needed to leave her husband: "I needed to save myself and my sanity, both of which were crumbling. I needed to be free."

A serious family argument prompted the following dream by a woman in her seventies. During a vacation visit, her brother became extremely angry over some minor event. During his outburst he made it very clear that he never wanted to see his sister again. Heartbroken, the sister returned home and wondered what she could do to heal their relationship. Because of previous incidents of this kind, other family members assured the woman that there was nothing she could do. Still, she hoped to resolve the situation, even though months had passed and her brother remained steadfast in his resolve to avoid all ties with the family.

> *I had this dream that my brother and I were in a shoe store. I wanted a pair of black patent leather Mary Janes, which I have never liked. The clerk said he only had one pair but that he also had a very pretty shade of brown in that same shoe. I looked down at my feet and discovered that I had four feet!*
>
> *I told the clerk that was fine, I could wear the brown ones on my back feet and they would not be too noticeable. My brother frowned, said that was ridiculous, and was very disgusted.*

The woman realized that the dream illustrated the confusion she felt about the direction she was supposed to take (four feet) in her relationship with her brother. She was so upset about the situation that she was willing to settle for any solution, even if it did not seem appropriate. The dream also suggested that no matter what she did, her brother would remain angry and critical. When a family member discovered that the brother had disconnected his phone without telling anyone his new number, the sister realized that her brother alone controlled the situation and there was really nothing she could do about it.

The following presents a final example of a dream that explores psychological issues. It involves a woman in her fifties who could not get a dream out of her head. She was so bothered by its vivid imagery that she sought assistance regarding its interpretation.

I was driving to my mother's house. When I got there, however, there was a mailman's truck in the driveway. I had to wait for him to move before I could pull in. When I finally pulled in the driveway, there were all these polar bears blocking the way. I had to park at an angle to get around them. When I started walking up the sidewalk to the door, there were more polar bears of all ages (babies, middle-aged, and old ones). I finally opened my mother's door and there was a bear rug lying on the floor. My mother was in the kitchen washing the dishes and I yelled in, "Mother, what are you doing with all these bears?" She yelled back, "They were on sale." That was the end of the dream.

When I heard this dream, the first thing I asked the woman was, "How do you feel about your mother?" Her reply was brusque. Her mother was deceased. She had never gotten along with the woman, and had felt "nothing" when she died. But the dream suggested otherwise.

During our conversation I suggested that an issue with her mother remained unresolved. The act of driving to her mother's house represents her relationship with her mother, the situation itself, or the fact that this was something she is headed for. There the dreamer confronts a message (mailman in the driveway). The thematic approach suggests that something is blocking someone, whether it is the mailman in the driveway or the bears scattered about the yard and house. This blockage is interfering with the communication between the dreamer and her feelings, or between the dreamer and her mother or both.

Polar bears are found in extremely cold climates filled with ice and snow. Ice and snow suggests "frozen emotions" or feelings that have been suppressed and held inside. In addition, a polar bear is one of nature's most aggressive creatures. Therefore the emotion being suppressed concerns her anger and aggression. Not being able to confront the situation directly, the dreamer apparently needs to address the problem from a different perspective.

The polar bears of all ages probably represent the repressed anger she has felt with her mother as a child, as a teenager, and as an adult. The bear rug right under her feet indicates that the situation can no longer be avoided because it is underfoot and directly in front of her.

That the mother is washing the dishes in the dream suggests a couple of possibilities. Either the relationship the dreamer has been served all of her life may be in the process of cleansing and healing. Or the frozen emotion (ice) is beginning to melt as the healing process begins. The deceased mother may also be working on trying to heal the situation from the other side. Her pronouncement that the bears are on sale might represent a thawing in their relationship, or that the dreamer has an opportunity to resolve the situation even though she is not conscious of her desire to heal the relationship.

At the end of our conversation I encouraged the dreamer to seek out a counselor to help her work through the situation. Though she claimed to feel nothing for her mother, the dream suggested that she really meant a great deal to her and that she had been seriously hurt by the relationship all her life. She could no longer repress the issue or let it go unresolved.

In addition to dreams for the body and dreams for the mind, each individual also experiences dreams for the soul. Sometimes these dreams deal with spiritual issues, and on other occasions the consciousness of the individual can actually come in contact with higher spiritual realities, experiencing what Edgar Cayce called "visions" in the dream-state. Dreams at this level can also involve past lives and precognitive information.

Cayce's own dream of being a speck of sand that was raised up in a whirlwind is one example of such a "visionary" experience. Often while giving a past-life reading, Cayce would see himself traveling through various levels of consciousness before arriving at an enormous universal library (the Akashic records). Here he would be met by an old man who would hand him a book – the soul record of the very individual for whom he was giving the reading.

Perhaps more common than visionary experiences are dreams that simply explore an individual's spiritual issues. In the first example, a reoccurring dream reflects a young man's search for personally meaningful spiritual information:

> *I find myself on a high ridge in the mountains where a bunch*
> *of pickup trucks are parked. People are sitting in chairs in the*
> *back of their pickups, fishing. They cast their lines far into the*
> *sky and hook these enormous trout! After catching the fish,*

they haul the fighting, flapping fish down and net them. It is a
very clear dream.

The mountains in this dream might represent the higher levels of the mind or the higher levels of spirituality. Generally, a pickup truck is regarded as an informal, comfortable, rugged, or manly form of transportation. So this imagery might indicate the young man's desire to find something appropriate and comfortable for himself spiritually. Casting lines into the sky can be associated with the exploration of various spiritual ideologies, beliefs, or thoughts. The dreamer is trying to "hook" the appropriate one. The fighting and flapping fish might suggest the dreamer's own struggle to come to terms with a personal belief system.

In another instance, a fifty-two-year-old woman raised in a very strict, conservative, and religious home "with lots of 'Thou shalt not's'" felt driven to discover a spiritual meaning in life. This dream seemed to portray both her personal search and her struggle to free herself from the past:

It is a reoccurring dream about climbing attic steps. I am try-
ing to get to the top but the fear of shadowy figures along my
path always scares me back down. I try to make the journey
over and over again. Finally, I am able to get to the attic and
find the interior of a church. It has lots of pews, stained glass
windows, and a pulpit in front.

The dream seems to mean that the woman has finally faced and overcome the issues that had been blocked her chances of experiencing a meaningful spiritual life. Once she found the church in the attic, her waking life was no longer troubled by thoughts of the fearful God with whom she had been raised.

Dreams for the soul might also involve past-life experiences. Such dreams are relatively common and generally have a present-day significance. Individuals do not randomly dream about the past. A past-life dream can be triggered by a present-day relationship or an issue that has its beginnings in the past, or it may be the result of a similar cycle occurring in the present, corresponding to something previously experienced by the soul. Historical places, clothing, people, or events in a dream can all suggest a past-life experience. The same is true of foreign cultures and international locales, or seeing one's self as a different person, a different sex, or with a different skin color. Repeatedly dreaming of a historical period or a culture means that the subconscious mind is drawing upon the images of a past-life experience as a way of relating present-day information.

A man in his fifties, who felt strongly drawn to Egypt although he had never been there, had a dream in which he witnessed a ceremony before thousands of people:

> *There was a great host of people going out to dedicate a tomb that was being built or prepared for someone, and they had seven days of entertainment with all sorts of dancing, prayer, and song. Just before the last service, I saw someone climb to the top of this pyramid or cone-like thing, and clang a big sheet of brass or metal of some kind. There were camels, beautiful drapes and hangings, and costumes of the period.*

In real life a psychic had told the dreamer that he was entering a period in his life when he would be drawn to people he had once known in Egypt. Apparently, many of the relationships that he had encountered in the past were resurfacing in the present. So it came as no surprise to the man when he suddenly found himself surrounded by friends and associates who felt a similar attraction to Egypt. While the imagery might have a basis in an actual past-life experience, it could also symbolize an initiation or some kind of ceremony, indicating that the dreamer was now experiencing a life cycle similar to one he had encountered in the past.

Past-life dreams sometimes use more contemporary imagery, as in this case of nineteen-year-old girl who seemed to dream about a past-life connection with a young man who was a friend in the present:

> *It was night and I was on a white horse with Daniel, riding out to a garden. We got off the horse, walked around, and found a place in the garden where we could lay down and look up at the stars.*

*The next scene I remember is riding the same white horse
with Daniel on the beach. We came upon these rocks, got off
the horse, and sat down to watch the dolphins play in the
ocean. In the dream, my hair was much longer than it really is,
my skin was a darker tan, and I was wearing some kind of a
dress that I don't own. Daniel looked pretty much the same but
his skin was also darker.*

In real life, the young woman had begun to have romantic feelings
about Daniel, a classmate at school. The dream suggested to her that her
feelings toward Daniel had roots in the past and that the two needed to
"finish what was started back then." Shortly after the dream, the two began
having a romantic relationship.

Precognitive dreams occur in various ways and provide the dreamer
with additional insights, warnings, or other previews of things to come. In
the case of this man in his forties, a dream offered an accurate depiction of
an accident at work:

*I saw one of my female coworkers, working on top of a pallet-
rack, as we occasionally did. For some reason, she must have
lost her balance and I was helpless as I watched her fall to the
ground.*

The next day, the man watched as the dream played out before his
eyes. His coworker, who was working on the pallet, suddenly fell about
eight feet from the top of the rack. Thankfully, she received only minor
injuries. But the dreamer was convinced that the fall might have been
averted had he thought to warn his coworker about his experience in time.

On another occasion, a businessman in his thirties had a dream that
indicated a change in his company's organization. His boss had left the
company and he was in line for the job. While waiting for the decision, he
had the following dream:

*I saw the table of organization on the company president's
desk. As if somehow watching over his shoulder, I saw the
president use a pencil eraser to erase the entire division that*

had once reported to my boss and separate it into two differ-
ent departments. Using his pencil, he then connected one of
the departments to an already existing division within the
company and then he connected the other department to
another division.

Within a week, the company announced that the departing division director would not be replaced. Instead, as a cost-savings measure, the company had decided to break apart the division and distribute its function among the company's existing divisions. As a result, the dreamer retained his job but ended up reporting to another division director.

In the following case, a woman in her thirties had a dream in which she saw herself communicating with deceased family members. But even in the dream, she realized that there was something unusual about the fact that one of her friends was also present for the occasion:

I saw myself traveling to (what I knew to be) the "other side." I
landed at a beautiful seaport and saw members of my
deceased family assembled. We gathered at a table as if for a
meal and seemed to be having a good time. I sat next to those I
was closest to. My grandfather gave me a letter to read but I
don't remember what it said. I suddenly realized that Edwin, a
good friend and neighbor, was also at the table. I was sur-
prised and wondered why he was there. After I gave a speech
about the importance of families the dream ended.

A short time after this dream, Edwin was diagnosed with terminal cancer and died at a very young age. The woman realized that somehow she had previewed his death amidst a gathering of deceased individuals she had loved.

In a final example, a mother in her forties with two grown sons has a visionary experience that helps her through a horrible family tragedy. This dream occurred while she was on vacation with her husband and baby granddaughter:

A friend of mine who I associate with spirituality came to me in a dream. She was dressed all in white and she told me that she wanted me to meditate on three things upon awakening: 1) Death is never an accident; 2) there are no coincidences; and, 3) only love is real.

When she awoke, she told her husband about the dream and reflected upon its three messages all day. The dream left her at peace and very much in touch with God. Later that day the call came from the hospital emergency room that her eldest son had been killed in a freak explosion and fire. Through the entire experience, she was never in a state of shock and never needed a sedative. Somehow the dream experience had prepared her for the impending tragedy.

The night after her son's death, as she was drifting off to sleep, she smelled fire and smoke. Suddenly she felt the presence of her deceased son who reached down and gave her "one of his bear hugs." The experience reinforced her belief that death was not an accident, that there was no such thing as coincidence, and that only love was real.

A universal truth about the human condition is that everyone dreams and that these dreams may involve physical problems or concerns, emotional or psychological issues, even matters of the spirit or soul. Dreams are important because they can showcase new insights, unresolved feelings, possible solutions, unexpressed aspirations, potential outcomes, and even possible past-life situations for the dreamer. Prompted by the subconscious mind, such dreams can help and assist individuals as they meet the demands and issues of everyday life. Because dreams are not limited to what we think we know, they possess an unlimited source of information. They are just there for the asking.

Chapter Six
Sample Dreams

(See Appendix 1 for possible interpretations.)

A. A forty-three-year-old woman is interested in spiritual development and her personal mission in life.

> *I dreamed I was driving home in my Jeep. In real life, to get to my house on the mountain I have to drive up a very steep hill for about a half-mile, then wind around the mountain. On the steep hill, there were several boulders – all perfectly round and smooth. They were scattered randomly. I continued to drive. As I reached the first boulder I cautiously peered around it, saw the way was clear, and continued on to the next boulder. There were one or two other cars on the hill that were stopped and couldn't go any further. I managed to weave around all the obstacles by driving up to them slowly, looking for an open path, finding one, and continuing to drive. Eventually, I reached the top of the hill.*

B. A young woman wants to return to college and focus on her career. Her husband is opposed to the idea and wants her to stay home with the kids.

> *I dreamed that I was walking along and noticed that a snake was biting my arm. I had to struggle to get it off my arm. Later, as I was walking, I noticed that a snake (could have been the same one) was biting my ankle.*

C. This man complains of feeling tired and lethargic and has trouble concentrating.

> *I dreamed that I was crazy and having problems thinking. Somehow I was able to look inside my head. With my skull open, I could see all kinds of gears and wheels spinning around in their proper place, except for one. One of the wheels had stopped running altogether because a particle of dirt or trash had gotten stuck in it.*

Unusual dreams and personal guidance

There are as many different kinds of dreams as there are individuals who experience them. All too often, unfortunately, people don't take the time to reflect upon their dreams upon awakening; the symbols and images become fragmented, dissipated and are soon forgotten – if they were ever even brought to mind at all. For some individuals, however, a dream can be so unusual and memorable that it is not easily shaken from memory. The substance of some dreams can even be molded and shaped by the dreamer once the dream is underway. In fact, taken a step further, most individuals do not realize that it is even possible to shape the direction and subject matter of one's dreams before going to sleep. This technique gives the dreamer access to answers on almost every imaginable question.

Take this example of a reoccurring dream that terrified a woman in her thirties. She was so frightened by it that she dreaded going to sleep and often awoke in a panic in the middle of the night. Even telling the dream seemed to make the woman somewhat fearful:

> *I am alone in my house. Although I am inside, I know that it is dusk and I begin to feel apprehensive. The apprehension grows as shadows are cast through the windows. I can't really see out, but the shadows come in. I begin looking for someone to help me but there is no one, and for some reason I cannot leave the house. I begin to hear whirling sounds as if something enormous is approaching overhead, like a helicopter. The sounds grows louder until the roof begins to shake and the ceiling begins to fall in because of the noise and the vibration. I become more afraid as I see the beams of the roof and then the sky. I panic when I realize that an enormous spaceship has*

come to get me. The spaceship hovers just over my head, a door begins to open, and a hideous creature comes out of the craft into my house. The creature approaches me and I am frozen with fear. Immediately, he begins to grope and touch me, putting his long, clammy fingers everywhere. I know I am going to be examined and raped. I go to scream but cannot make a sound. I usually wake up in a panic.

As the dreamer recounted her dream, I watched her become increasingly fearful, fidgety, and apprehensive. I was only partially listening as the dreamer expressed her concern that she had even begun to wonder whether or not she was being abducted by aliens. Certainly the imagery suggested that something was overpowering her and she had no control over it. When we began talking about her life, her family, and her work, nothing seemed to correspond to the dream. Just as I was planning to explore the symbolism with her, the woman wondered aloud, "Why would I keep having a dream like this?"

"Well, sometimes," I casually replied, "individuals who have unresolved life experiences, such as fears, regrets, or abuse can have those very same issues come up in their dreams."

The dreamer immediately began to cry. I tried to comfort her but her cries did not stop until she sighed and said, "I know what it's about." The woman then began to tell a horrendous story about the sexual abuse she had suffered as a child at the hands of her father. Clearly the dream reflected those same issues: the fact that evening brought about a child's feelings of apprehension, the lack of potential rescuers, the overpowering feelings, and so forth. After telling her story, the dreamer admitted that she had thought she had already worked through all of the issues surrounding her childhood ordeal. The two of us agreed that they obviously had not been resolved and she promised to seek out additional counseling.

Another frightening dream affected a twenty-year-old man who was extremely busy with college and work. Because of his hectic schedule, he rarely got enough sleep. The dream usually occurred during those equally rare short, afternoon naps:

I am lying on my bed. Even though my eyes are closed, I feel like I am awake and I am conscious of everything in the room.

I can even "see" and "hear" but I am still in bed. Suddenly I start to feel a very strong pressure on my chest, arms, and legs as if someone or something is pushing me into the bed. I try to say something but my mouth won't open and I am unable to move my body. Sometimes I can hear someone out in the hall-way – and if I check with that person later, he or she was really there – but I cannot call out. I feel totally paralyzed and I become afraid. It takes a while before I am back to normal and able to really get up.

I have heard dozens of variations on this same dream from men and women of all ages, so I reassured the dreamer that his experience was relatively common. I don't think this was simply a dream, however, but an "out of body" experience that occurs in the hypnagogic, or half-asleep half-awake, state.

According to Edgar Cayce, consciousness is not confined to the physical body. Therefore, during a dream, it is possible for one's consciousness to "leave" the body, sometimes hovering just above it. When an experience like this occurs, the individual somehow becomes conscious while she or he is out of body. The individual can still "see," "hear," "rationalize," and on occasion even "smell," but has absolutely no control over these sensations because the individual is no longer in his or her physical body. Until consciousness returns, the person remains "paralyzed."

I told the young man what to do the next time it happened. It is apparently possible to shorten the experience by either focusing your consciousness on your forehead, starting a prayer, or trying to move a body part (such as a finger). At least that is what has assisted many individuals who have had the same type of experience.

Lucid dreams also suggest that consciousness exists beyond the physical body. Simply stated, lucid dreaming occurs whenever an individual becomes conscious of dreaming while in the dream-state and finds that he or she can mold, shape, change, or otherwise direct the content of the dream. Such a dream offers the individual an opportunity to have a very meaningful and enlightening experience if they chose to take advantage of it.

One of my favorite lucid dream stories occurred to a young man of twenty three. He told me that his flying dreams often turned into lucid dreams. Generally, he used the experience to feel the exhilaration of flight, or to travel to somewhere he had never been in his waking life. Since he was raised as a Christian, I encouraged him to try something different next time. I told him, "The next time you become lucid, say that you want to speak with Jesus." A few weeks passed before the young man shared a dream with the rest of the class:

> *I was flying in the clouds like I have done before. Suddenly, I became aware of the fact that I was dreaming. I was about to go flying again when I remembered what Kevin had said in class about doing something spiritual. Instead of flying I stopped in the air, looked around at the sky and said aloud, "I want to speak with Jesus."*
>
> *All at once a shaft of light tore through the sky and began drawing the shape of a door. When the door was complete, a very bright light began to shine on all four sides of the door and streams of light began pouring out from under it. Slowly, the door started opening, causing the brightest light I have ever seen to begin pouring out.*
>
> *As I watched this I started to become very afraid. The door kept opening and I started to worry. Before the door could open any further, I screamed, "I changed my mind, I changed my mind!"*

The dreamer awoke quite apprehensive about the dream, but the class laughed hysterically when they heard it. If only he had been brave enough to continue the dream, he might have had a truly remarkable experience.

Another memorable dream occurred in the life of a woman in her fifties who contacted me a week after the horrible Oklahoma City bombing. She felt guilty, confused, and overwhelmed because of a dream she had experienced. The dream seemed to preview the destruction of the nine-story Alfred P. Murrah Federal Building:

> *I was in some kind of a daycare center that was in an office building at least six stories tall. I was watching the children playing and everything seemed to be fine when suddenly there was a tremendous explosion. The blast ripped through the*

room, causing the children to be thrown against the wall. As the bodies flew, I knew most of them were dead. I turned to look at my own injuries which seemed to be mostly cuts and scrapes on my arms.

The dream occurred several days before the bombing and caused the dreamer intense guilt. "Maybe I could have prevented it or warned someone somehow, " she explained. Even though the dreamer lived near Atlanta and the dream had not specified any location for the bombing or given any details about the building, she still felt that her inaction made her somehow responsible. This sense of guilt is not unique for such dreams. Sometimes these dreams involve plane crashes or earthquakes, and on other occasions they deal with murder, robbery, or assault. Dreamers often wonder why they have experienced such a dream and what they were supposed to have done to prevent it.

A dreamer can only be expected to follow-through on those things that he or she is capable of accomplishing. In other words, there is quite a difference between warning a friend to watch his or her driving, and trying to locate which cities have daycare centers in buildings with more than six floors in order to warn them in time. Individuals who experience such dreams are not necessarily supposed to do anything about them. (A dream of this nature can always be seen as a call to prayer for all those concerned.) They occur because the dreamer has somehow become attuned to the situation in question, either because of their heightened intuitive perception, or because the situation resonated with some activity in the dreamer's own life.

I asked the woman who had this dream, what if the bombing had not occurred? What might the dream then mean for her personally? In talking with her, I discovered that she was a schoolteacher who had "burned out" after serving nearly thirty-years in elementary school education. Although part of her loved teaching and young children, she no longer felt strong enough to deal with the type of behavior of the children that were now a part of her classroom. "Children aren't the same as they used to be," she said, "and I'm just too old to deal with it." But she was sad about her retirement because she had truly loved her work.

I saw several reasons why she may have experienced this horrible dream. Simple intuition was one possibility. Just as she empathized with the children in the bombing and yet could do nothing to help them, so she had truly felt for her own students even though she could no longer effectively deal with them. In terms of dream imagery, the devastation of the daycare center might correspond with leaving her job in elementary education, an event which effectively blew her whole world apart. She had also been injured, at least emotionally, as a teacher (cuts and scrapes).

A similar dream by a nine-year-old girl dealt with another tragedy:

> *Two weeks before the spaceship Challenger blew up I had a dream that it did. When I saw the plume of smoke from the explosion on the TV, it looked the same as the plume of smoke in my dream. I was only in the third grade at the time and the experience really scared me. When I saw it on TV I felt like I could have done something to prevent it, but who is going to believe a little kid saying that the Challenger is going to blow up. The strangest thing about it was that Christa, the schoolteacher aboard had the same first name as I do.*

Certainly a nine-year-old child would have never been able to prevent the tragedy. The dream obviously occurred as a result of the dreamer's intuition and her own feelings of a connection with Christa McAuliffe. If there was a symbolic connection to the dreamer's waking life, the dreamer, now a young woman, could not think of any.

Most individuals who work with their dreams know they can get insightful and helpful guidance though dream interpretation. Unusual dreams can also provide guidance. The following two examples illustrate this point. The first is the dream of a young woman who averted a potential accident for one of her children.

When she became pregnant with her second child, she told her two-and-a-half-year-old daughter, "Since the baby is going to sleep in your crib, you're now old enough to have a big bed." Shortly thereafter the woman and her husband purchased a full-size bed for their daughter and placed it up against her bedroom wall. That night she had this experience:

> *The first night my daughter slept in her "big bed," my husband and I placed chairs against the open side of the bed in order to keep her from falling to the floor. That night when I*

was asleep I dreamed that she was calling for me. For some reason, she was in trouble. I immediately awakened and went to check on her.

When the woman entered her daughter's room, she found that the child had rolled out of bed and was hanging precariously between the two chairs, but still very much asleep. The dream had simply been a warning to go and help the child.

The second dream involves a middle-aged man whose wife of nearly twenty years had surprised him with the news that she no longer loved him. He had not only supported her emotionally and financially while she had earned her two degrees, but they had become partners in business together. Just as their marriage, future, and financial wherewithal seemed better than ever, the wife had requested a divorce. "I was devastated," said her husband. "I couldn't sleep and I couldn't eat. This was the closest I ever came to a nervous breakdown." Over the next few months he lost thirty-five pounds because of his depression and emotional state.

His friends tried to help him through the emotional turmoil. Some people told him that he would probably look back on his divorce as a blessing; since his marriage had been far from perfect, now he would have the opportunity to start over. Despite such encouragement, the man still wanted his wife back. One night he awoke from a dream aware that getting back together with his wife was not the thing to do. While still in the hypnagogic state he had the following unusual experience:

I knew that I was at a crossroads. It was a point of choosing. I seemed to be viewing things from a superconscious state. I was completely unemotional in this state and viewed the choices set before me. The story of "the Lady" or "the Tiger" seemed to be the choice. If I chose "the Lady" I was choosing "Lady Luck," taking my chances with what life had to offer and being free to do God's work. I knew this choice meant financial prosperity. It also meant joy and happiness.

However, if I chose "the Tiger," meaning my wife, it would mean many years of counseling and of working things out. An insight came to me that hanging on to my wife was hanging on to ego.

Once fully awake the man realized that divorce was truly the best thing for him.

A very unusual example of dream guidance that involved the Edgar Cayce readings took place in 1977, more than thirty years after Cayce's death. A middle-aged woman in New Zealand was suffering from a series of health problems. She experienced dizziness and fainting spells, felt pain in her side, and often complained of problems with her liver, kidneys, and bladder. Her doctor could not determine the cause of her condition and treated her for low blood sugar and an imbalance of red and white blood cells. But her symptoms persisted and she felt miserable.

Finally, a friend suggested that she pray for guidance, which she did. One night she had a dream in which she saw herself looking at one of Edgar Cayce's readings. She could see that the case history was number 1880. When she told her friends about her dream, they wrote to Cayce's Association for Research and Enlightenment in Virginia Beach, Virginia and requested a copy of the reading for case 1880. When the reading arrived several weeks later, she was amazed to find that the individual who had requested the reading in 1939 had complained of the same symptoms she was experiencing. Edgar Cayce had told the individual in 1939 that the cause of the problem was mercury poisoning. He then went on to outline a treatment regimen.

After learning of this, the woman contacted her mother and asked: "Was I ever exposed to mercury as a child?" Yes, replied her mother, quite surprised; she had once bitten off the end of a thermometer and swallowed its contents. Armed with this information, the dreamer asked her doctor to test her for mercury. When the doctor refused, the woman found another doctor who agreed to perform the test. And she tested positive.

This second doctor thought the mercury poisoning was not due to her childhood accident but to the medications she had been taking. Nonetheless, the woman began following the treatment outlined in the Cayce reading and within a few months all of her symptoms had disappeared.

Individuals are often surprised to learn that they can be proactive in obtaining dream guidance. It is possible to access the insights from one's subconscious mind simply by asking. All you have to do is write out a question before going to bed, read it once or twice before turning out the lights and drifting off to sleep, and then simply allowing your dreams to provide insights into virtually anything. I have collected many example of this simple approach over the years.

An middle aged man who had been studying spiritual philosophies for several years wrote out this question, "What do I need to work on spiritually?" That night he had the following dream:

> *I was walking next to some old buildings in a quaint little town. All at once I realized I was walking next to an individual I considered to be very spiritual. I stopped, looked up at the person and asked, "So how am I doing?" as if to inquire about my spiritual progress. He looked at me, pulled his glasses down his nose a little, peered over the lenses and said, "We'll, you know, you do spend more time watching TV then you do meditating."*

The dreamer took the dream to mean that he needed to spend less time studying and reading about spiritual things and more time meditating and applying what he had been reading.

In another example, a middle-aged woman who asked about whether or not she should take a job that she had been offered had the following dream:

> *I dreamed that I was looking at a shiny new car in the show-room on a car lot. It was beautiful and I decided that I wanted it. I tried to get into the car but there was no key. When I finally found a salesperson with the key, the car wouldn't start. When the car was fixed and finally started, I couldn't get the car in gear – the car rolled backwards off of its platform in the showroom, crashing through the showroom window and into the parking lot. I quickly got out of the car and suddenly the hood opened and the engine rose out of the car and started heading towards me. I ran off in a panic.*

Because of this dream, the dreamer did not take the job. She associated the new job with the shiny new car in the dream and decided that there were all kinds of unforeseen problems with the job. She was certain that she would regret taking it.

On another occasion, a man in his twenties, weary of his current employment, wrote out the question, "When will I get a new job?" After attempting the process for two nights, he had this memorable dream:

I am a waiter like I was back in college. I am standing next to my side station, where they keep the plates, glasses, and silverware, busily cleaning up my section. I know that I have to get everything in order because I will be starting a new job in six weeks. That was the end of the dream.

Taking the information at face value, the dreamer began putting his work in order. After catching up on tasks he had been neglecting, he "waited" to see what job might present itself. Three weeks later, he came across a new position that appealed to him. Although he had no previous experience in the line of work, he applied for it anyway. Several others had also applied for the job but he was not discouraged. He breezed through the interview and was offered the job. He then gave his old boss two weeks notice. As the dream had foretold, *he started his new job six weeks after having the dream!*

In the next case an individual wanted to know why his life was such a challenge. So he wrote out on a piece of paper, "What is the connection between this experience and my soul's purpose?" That night he had this dream:

I dreamed I was sitting at the breakfast table with my wife. Suddenly, I notice a piece of paper sticking out of my pocket. I reach down, open it up, and see that it has one word written on it: "enlightenment."

To the dreamer, this meant that his challenges were actually learning experiences, that they were somehow helping him become a better person.

Lastly, one of the most memorable examples of someone asking a question and getting an answer occurred in the case of a woman in her thirties whose three-year-old daughter, Terry, had been killed in a car accident. Depressed and devastated, the woman had no belief in an afterlife, a belief that might have helped her through the tragedy.

A friend asked me to talk with this woman. During our conversation, I explained that since consciousness was not limited to the confines of the physical body, it was possible to communicate with a deceased loved one during the dream-state. Since she was extremely upset by the thought that her daughter had simply ceased to exist, I encouraged her to write out the question, "How is Terry doing?" and to bring me any dream that she might have. A few days later the woman called to say, "I have a dream but it doesn't make any sense!" She then told me this dream:

I went to the cemetery and to the grave where Terry was buried. When I got there, I saw Terry sitting all by herself on top of the grave with a birthday cake and some lit candles. She looked up at me, smiled, and said, "Don't worry mommy, I'm okay. I'm okay." I started crying, which woke me up.

When I told the woman that her dream was a beautiful one, she replied, "But she's not okay, she's dead!" I explained that although her daughter was no longer physical, she was still very much alive. I expressed my firm belief that real communication had actually taken place between the two of them.

Dreams are much more than fantasy, make believe, or the imaginative wondering of one's consciousness. They are more than the nighttime receptacle of an individual's thoughts, issues, experiences, and concerns played out against the background of subconscious symbols and images. They are an exploration into the deepest recesses of consciousness, giving individuals insights into repressed issues and desires, exploring current events and relationships, supplying them with practical guidance and straightforward advice, and providing a glimpse of the future or an alternative state of consciousness. The guidance and direction available in the sleep-state are apparently limitless. Wouldn't it be nice if those same subconscious insights were accessible during waking consciousness?

They can be.

Chapter Seven
Sample Dreams

(See Appendix 1 for possible interpretations.)

A. A woman in her forties who works at a bank in Norfolk, Virginia, had this dream:

> *I saw Norfolk, Virginia from the air. I could see the naval shipyard and downtown. Suddenly a missile descended from the sky and struck the ground near the waterside. Before anyone could realize what had happened, the city was annihilated and an enormous mushroom cloud rose high up into the air.*

B. A thirty-year-old man was close to his grandfather, who died six weeks before this dream:

> *A few weeks after my Grandfather died, I began having a reoccurring dream about him. In the dream there was some kind of a large family gathering like Thanksgiving. Everyone was gathered around the table in the kitchen for dinner. I happened to look through the door that led into the living room and saw my Grandfather, who I knew was dead, sitting on the couch all by himself. I was the only one who could see him. I went and sat by him on the couch and started talking with him.*
>
> *My grandfather told me that he was all right and doing just fine. He also thanked me and stated that he had really enjoyed being my grandfather. He gave me a hug and we talked some more. The experience was very uplifting and yet the whole time the rest of my family remained completely oblivious to my grandfather's presence and just went on with their dinner.*

C. A man in his sixties wrote out the question, "What do I need to work on spiritually?" before going to sleep. This dream followed:

I dreamed that I was in the army (I have never been in the army) and I was some kind of a drill sergeant doing important paperwork. My desk was filled with important papers and things that were scheduled – everything was neatly organized and in its proper place. Suddenly a younger man came into my office unannounced. He was singing and dancing and appeared to be having a very good time with himself. To my surprise, he jumped up on top of my desk and started tap dancing all over my paperwork. Everything that I had neatly organized was in disarray. After making a thorough mess, the man continued to sing and dance right out of my office. Immediately, I picked up the phone and called security and yelled into the received, "I want that man arrested, and I want to know who he is!" I slammed the phone down, very angry for the interruption. Suddenly, security came into my office bringing the man who had caused the disruption. They announced that they had caught him and that he was "the company clown."

CHAPTER 8

Conscious dreamplay

Individuals are much more aware of themselves – their skills, weaknesses, challenges, and surroundings – than they think. Like a complex radar system, the human mind constantly collects data and information that can be drawn upon for any situation at any time. To be sure, most of this acquired information is never brought to conscious awareness. Instead it remains within the subconscious, emerging only as feelings, hunches, insights, and intuition. Although the human mind utilizes, at least subconsciously, all of the information coming to it, some studies suggest that of all the data collected by an individual's mind, less than five percent ever truly becomes conscious.

Though this percentage might sound low, how aware we are we really of everything around us? How often are we aware of the sounds of our heating and air conditioning systems? Do we always feel the touch of our clothing against our skin? Do we acknowledge the breathing sounds made by someone standing next to us in an elevator? Are we conscious of the feeling of the seat on which we are sitting, the weight of our glasses upon our nose, or the fit of our shoes against our feet? How often do we drive to work and then have no conscious knowledge of the trip that actually took us there? Do we ever hear the sounds of the tires beneath our cars? Little of this information ever reaches conscious awareness. So, what happens to it?

The answer is that all of the data, information, and sense perceptions that are acquired by the mind become stored in the subconscious. It is for this reason that individuals who witness a crime scene are often able to remember greater details under hypnosis than they might have recalled consciously. No information is ever forgotten; it is just stored in a place we do not normally know how to access.

Not only does the subconscious have a seemingly limitless storage capacity, but it is also a primary facilitator of personal intuition. Because consciousness at this level is not limited by physicality, there are no boundaries to block personal awareness. Things we often refer to as "hunches," "gut feelings," or some kind of special "knowing" can all originate at this level. In this same manner, professional intuitives are somehow able to tap the resources of their subconscious mind and respond to questions with answers of which they have no conscious knowledge.

Due to the wealth of information stored within the subconscious mind, dreams are able to provide an abundance of insight, guidance, and personal direction. But what if this information was not limited to the sleep-state? What if these insights were not just available to professional intuitives but to everyone in their lives? What if an individual could somehow bypass the limitations of her or his conscious mind and access information directly from the subconscious? To be sure, the information would be in the form of symbols, the language of the brain, but could it be accessed and would it be helpful?

This question has led a number of individuals to develop various approaches to something called "intuitive imagery," "creative imagery," or simply the "imagination game."[3] All approaches simply entail creating a real question that the individual desires an answer or insight to, providing the conscious mind with a decoy focus, and then accessing valid symbolic insights from the subconscious mind. Because the end result of the process resembles a dream and needs to be interpreted like a dream, I call the experience "Conscious Dreamplay."

This game has countless variations and can be played alone or with others. Just like a dream, it can provide insights into an individual's life, work, relationships, challenges, and future. Once a real question (for the subconscious mind) and a decoy question (for the conscious mind) has been established, the individual should relax and begin imagining whatever the conscious mind has been asked to focus upon. (A sample relaxation exercise can be found in Appendix 2.) For ease of explanation, what

---

3 Proponents of intuitive imagery include: Magaly del Carmen Rodriguez, consultant to *Fortune 100* companies, and her work with creative imaging; Annie Gottlieb and Slobodan D. Pesic, authors of *The Cube. . .Keep the Secret*; and, John B. Pehrson and Susan E. Mehrtens, authors of *Intuitive Imagery: A Resource at Work.*

follows is one woman's experience from a workshop I led:

A woman in her fifties wanted to know if the time had come to leave her present employer. She wrote out the question, "Is it time to leave my job?" on a small piece of paper. She folded it so that no one could see the question, and handed it to another member of the conference. This question became the "real" question she wanted her partner's subconscious mind to work on and provide insights.

When everyone in the audience had written their question, folded it so that no one could see it, and handed the question to a partner, I took everyone through a short relaxation exercise and then asked the participants to imagine, "*A scene, a place of any kind. It can be a scene that you make up or one that truly exists. What do you see?*" This became the question for the conscious mind. The scene would symbolically represent whatever question each individual held in his or her hand. This thought was actually the real question for the subconscious mind of the person doing the imagining.

Next, I asked all participants to imagine that they were meeting someone wonderful: "*Meet someone wonderful. Who do you see? How do you feel about this person?*" (Conscious mind.) This someone would symbolize an aspect of the individual who had asked the real question and might be helpful in answering his or her own question. (Subconscious mind.)

Finally, I told all participants that this someone had something to give them: "*This person has something to give you. What is it?*" (Conscious mind.) This something would help the individual who had asked the real question answer his or her own question. (Subconscious mind.)

When the process was complete, and all individuals had written their imagined scenes, people, and objects on the original folded question, the questions were unfolded and the person doing to the imagining tried to interpret the images he or she had seen in relation to the actual question. The partner of the woman in her fifties had seen the place, Quito, Ecuador, met the person, Walt Disney, and had been handed Walt's watch.

In the process of interpreting the images, the partner said that he associated Quito, Ecuador, with the equator. In Quito, he said, there is a place where an individual can stand with one foot in the Southern Hemisphere and the other in the Northern Hemisphere. Relating this image to the question, the partner felt it indicated that the woman had "feet in two different worlds" (e.g. leaving her job or staying).

The partner felt that the person of Walt Disney suggested "creativity and boundless potential." Both of these elements were lacking in the woman's present job, prompting her, in part, to seek new employment. She did not feel that all of her talents and abilities were being put to use. The watch's symbolism was obvious. It was a response to the woman's original question, "Is it time to leave my job?" and the answer was, "It's time!"

All of these insights prove particularly amazing when you consider the fact that the woman's partner had no prior knowledge of the real question.

Here are some step-by-step instructions for playing the imagination game with others:

1) Formulate a question you would like an answer to. Write out the real question so that only you can see it. You can ask it anyway you wish, but a question phrased, "What is the energy (or possibilities) surrounding the new job offer?" will be easier to interpret than "If I get the new job, will I like it and will it allow me to utilize my talents?"

2) Create a decoy question that the conscious mind of the "imaginer" (the person trying to visualize the image) can focus upon. This question should be something easy to imagine, such as "See a package," "See a structure," "See a person," "See a painting," "See a movie," "See a scene," etc. This question becomes the "decoy question" receiving the attention of the conscious mind of the individual doing the imagining. Because intuition originates at the subconscious, that same individual's subconscious mind will be tuning into the real question, providing symbols and images that correspond to it.

As the game progresses, you can add additional decoy questions for greater insights into the real situation: "See a structure...what do you see?" "Something is going on inside the structure, what is it?" "How do you feel about this structure and what you see?" "If you could rate this picture from one to ten (ten being the best), how would you rate it?" etc. All of these additional images can be interpreted in relation to the real question after the conscious dreamplay experience is complete.

3) If you are leading a group of individuals through this process, your real questions need to be generic enough so that they can correspond with each individual's personal question. For example, your "See a structure" (decoy question), would correspond to something like: "Let the imaginer see an image of the questioner's real question" (real question). The secondary question, "Something is going on inside the structure, what is it?" might be associated with "Is there a way of seeing more clearly into this situation," and so forth. If you are leading a group, it is important for your mind to focus on the real question even though you are verbalizing the decoy question. You may also wish to have the real question written in a place where only you can see it. On the other hand, if you are playing the game with only one other person, you can simply ask the decoy question and then think the real question immediately thereafter.

4) After the conscious dreamplay imagination experience is complete, you can then interpret any images received against the real question.

On another occasion, a woman in her twenties wanted to know if a job prospect she had heard about was worth pursuing. Using the same decoy questions that involved seeing a scene, seeing a person, and being given something, what follows is her experience:

I wrote out the question, "Is the job in Houston worth looking into?" I folded my piece of paper and handed it to my partner, who had no idea what I was asking. After the imagination exercise, my partner told me that she had seen a scene in which two ornate double doors opened onto a beautiful garden. The person she met was an old boyfriend that she had broken up with a long time ago and he handed her a ring.

In interpreting the images, my partner and I decided that the double doors indicated that the job was worth pursuing. The doorway meant that this job could be the doorway to some beautiful experience, where I'll be able to use my talents, indicated by the garden. After discussing it for a little while, she told me that she had really been attracted to this boyfriend but he had never wanted to make a commitment to her so they had broken up. We decided that the boyfriend's offer of a ring symbolized one of two possibilities. Either this job will be ideally suited for me, like a marriage, or I will really like the job and it might even lead to a new relationship for me.

I think the job is definitely worth pursuing!

On another occasion, an employer in the travel business used a variation of this conscious dreamplay exercise when a problem arose at work. Vicki, one of his travel agents, came into his office expressing concern that Darlene, the twenty-two-year-old staff person assigned to accompany the tour to Egypt, had suddenly been forbidden to go on the tour by her father. Apparently Darlene's father was concerned about political events in the country. Since the tour was scheduled to leave in four days, the employer had a problem. Who was he going to send on the tour? His own schedule did not allow a change of plans. Without explaining anything to Vicki, he told her that he wanted to play an "imagination game" to help solve the problem. What follows is the variation of the game he used:

I instructed Vicki to sit down, close her eyes, and take a deep breath so that she could begin to relax.

While she was relaxing, I wrote out my real question at the top of my page, "Who is going to Egypt?" Logically, I thought that there were only three choices. Since I couldn't go, the options were Darlene, Vicki, or Angela, another woman in the office. I figured that I might be able to call Darlene's father and convince him that the trip was safe. Another option was Vicki, who had a lot of previous experience traveling on very short notice. The final logical choice was Angela, who had told me several times that one day she wanted to see the pyramids.

Beneath my real question, I decided to draw three doors, one right next to the other, to set up the decoy question. Beneath each of the doors I wrote a name: Darlene, Vicki, and Angela, in that order.

When Vicki was relaxed, I told her, "I want you to see three doors." I waited for a moment and then said, "Describe the first door to me." The real question I was thinking is, "How about sending Darlene to Egypt?"

Vicki explained that she could see a wooden door that was bolted shut with an enormous chain across it. I asked her to try and open the door and see what was behind it, and she replied, "There's nothing there." Finally, I asked her to rate the picture she had seen between one and ten, with ten being the highest, she gave it a four.

Next, I asked her to see the third door, to open it, and to describe what was behind it. The real question I was thinking is, "How about sending Angela to Egypt?" She said, "I see a very attractive door. It's a very rich looking color, like royal purple. I really like this door. Behind it I can see a rolling countryside. There are beautiful trees and meadows." The rating she gave the image was a seven.

Finally, I asked her to describe the middle door and what was behind it. The real question I was thinking is, "How about sending Vicki to Egypt?" She replied, "The door is the color of alabaster, like an old column in a temple. Behind it I can see brilliant sunlight, beautiful palm trees, and stretches and stretches of sand. The rating I give it is a nine-and-a-half."

Since the employer associated the first door that was locked and had nothing behind it to Darlene, he decided that the imagery was suggesting that Darlene's father had made up his mind (it was locked) and there was "nothing" the employer could say to get him to change it. Although the third door, associated with Angela, appeared very attractive at first, it was not as impressive as the center door, corresponding to Vicki. Even the imagery seemed to suggest that Vicki was going to Egypt. Because of the experience, the employer decided that Vicki was the one to accompany the tour. As a result of the exercise, Vicki went to Egypt with the tour and she and the group had a wonderful experience.

Interestingly enough, back home halfway through the tour, Angela's mother was taken unexpectedly to the hospital for emergency open-heart surgery. The employer decided that was the reason the exercise had chosen Vicki to go to Egypt rather than Angela. Somehow Vicki's subconscious mind had known that Angela would need to remain behind to be with, and help, her mother.

It is also possible to play the conscious dreamplay exercise alone. Since the questioner and the individual doing the imagining are the same, the conscious mind has to be given several decoy questions so that it does not impose its feelings, thoughts, and desires on the symbolism for the real question. Here is one possible approach to playing the game by yourself:

1) Formulate a question you would like an answer to. Place three 5 x 8 cards (or identical pieces of paper) on the table in front of you. On one of the cards write out the real question for which you are interested in receiving insights. Because you need to create a decoy for the conscious mind, on each of the other two cards write out a phony question. Phony questions can be things that you really want an answer to, or simple questions such as, "What is the energy surrounding this weekend?" "How will I feel about this particular movie?" etc. When each of the cards has a question written on it, fold them or turn them all upside down so that you are no longer able to see what question is on which card. Mix all of the cards on top of the table so that you don't know where any question has ended up.

2) Create a decoy question that your conscious mind can focus upon. This question should be something easy to imagine, such as "See a door," "See a structure," "See a person," "See a package," "See a movie," "See a house," etc. This question becomes the "focus question" receiving your conscious attention. Your subconscious mind will be able to tune into the hidden real question, providing symbols and images that correspond to it.

Place your hand on one of the cards and begin to focus on the decoy question. During the process you can add additional decoy questions for greater insights into the real situation: "See a person…who do you see?" "This person has just finished a particular project, what is it?" "If this person could give you a message, what would it be?" "If you could rate this picture from one to ten (ten being the best), how would you rate it?" and so forth.

3) When you have completed the imagination experience for one card, write down all of the images you saw on the back of that card. Move on to the next card, repeating the imagination game for each of the cards. Do not turn over any of the cards until you have completed this process for each of your questions, the one real question and the two phony questions.

4) After the conscious dreamplay imagination experience is complete for all three cards, interpret each of the images received against the questions written on the other side of the card.

Using this exercise, a woman in her thirties wanted to know about her job prospects. As part-time consultant, she did not make as much as she needed and had started looking for full-time work. She wrote out three questions (one real and two phony) on the back of three different cards. Although we could certainly interpret the imagery associated with each of her three questions, two of them were relatively unimportant. Her real question was "What are the chances of my getting a new job soon?" This was her experience:

My real question was "What are my chances of getting a new job soon?" I wrote out two other questions having to do with the current week and my family. Afterwards, I turned each of the cards over, shuffled them in front of me, relaxed, and closed me eyes.

I decided to imagine seeing someone for each of the cards. One at a time, I imagined seeing an individual, describing that person, sensing how I felt about that individual, and having the person give me something. When the experience was over, I went through and tried to interpret each of the images.

The image that corresponded with my real question was Mr. Magoo. I saw Mr. Magoo standing and squinting, unable to see in front of him. I felt like I really liked him even thought he was not able to clearly see me. When I imagined him giving me something, it turned out to be a big sack of money. I rated the image an eight.

After the experience, the woman decided that Mr. Magoo suggested that there was something right in front of her that she was unable to see. But that something was going to be very lucrative (sack of money) and she was really going to like it (rating = eight). As a result of the image, she tried to put her worries to rest and to keep her "eyes open" instead. A few weeks later, a company that she had consulted for offered her a full-time job. The money was good, even better than she had expected. Apparently the job had been open for quite some time, but neither the employer nor the woman had been able to immediately "see" that she had been a perfect fit for the position.

On another occasion, a man in his thirties was undecided about whether or not a particular stock would be a good investment. As in the preceding example, he wrote out his three questions, the real one dealing with the stock purchase. He decided that to "See a building" would be his decoy question and had the following experience:

My question was "Is this stock a good investment for me at this time?" I wrote this question on one card and two additional questions on two different cards. I turned all the cards over and rearranged their order so that I would not know where any of the questions were.

I imagined that I could "See a building" for each of the cards. My secondary decoy question was "Something is occurring in the building; what is it?" When the imagination part of the game was complete and I had written some notes about my visualization on the back of each card, I turned all of the cards face up.

For my real question, the building I had seen was the World Trade Center, which I associate with business success. The activity inside the building was a big party, involving hundreds of employees. I could see balloons and streamers, some of the employees even had noisemakers like a New Year's Eve party. It was a real celebration.

I decided that the image was showing me that the stock would meet with great success and that I would truly celebrate my purchase. I went ahead and bought the stock.

There are any number of variations to the conscious dreamplay exercise. One variation involves several individuals sitting around a table and writing out their real questions. The pieces of paper are then folded (so that no one can see the real questions), collected, and shuffled. Each person around the table then draws one of the papers without looking at the question. It does not matter if an individual gets her or his question, because the conscious mind will not know and the subconscious mind will be able to access appropriate insights regardless of which question is being answered.

One member of the group then asks a series of generic decoy questions for everyone. "See a place," "Meet someone," "See a painting," and "Describe a scene," are all examples of questions that might begin the process. As before, additional decoy questions can be asked to acquire additional insights into the real question. Another option is to have each individual think of decoy questions. Regardless of which approach is used, when the exercise is over, each individual will take turns reading the real question she or he drew aloud. After reading the question, the individual will then discuss what was seen in response to the decoy question. Afterwards, everyone around the table can work together to interpret the imagined images in terms of the real question.

One example of playing the conscious dreamplay game in a group involves a woman in her fifties who wanted to inquire about the health of her father, who was a widower. Her father was getting older and he often talked about his desire to rejoin his wife. One day the daughter decided to play the imagination game with some friends. She wrote out her question, "How much longer will my father be with me?" All the questions were then shuffled and each person drew one. This was the woman's experience:

I did not know whose question I had drawn, but the first thing we did as a group was, "See a painting." The painting was supposed to give us insights into what the real question was all about. All at once, I saw a painting of a beautiful Christmas tree with lights. In order to discover additional insights into the question, we each imagined that we 'snapped' our finger and watched what happened to the painting. Suddenly, the Christmas tree became real and was covered in brilliant white lights. We next imaged an individual who could help us solve our question. All at once I saw my deceased mother who stood there smiling at me lovingly. The final decoy image was to have this individual hand us something – again as a means of solving the question. In response to the question, my mother reached out and handed me an angel ornament, like you would take off a Christmas tree.

When it came time for the woman to read aloud the real question she had drawn she was amazed to see that she had picked her own question. The woman told the group that she loved Christmas and always considered it to be a special time of year. Like most people, she associated her mother with love, and the angel to spirituality and heaven.

The group then compared the images to her real question, "How much longer will my father be with me?" They decided that one possible meaning was that her father would die shortly after Christmas. For that reason, the woman was encouraged to make Christmas with him a very special occasion.

Christmas came and went without incident and the woman did all she could to make the season a joyful experience for her father. Then in the first week of January the woman called her friends to tell them that her father had died suddenly, but peacefully, in his sleep.

Another group variation of this exercise calls for the individual guiding the participants to decide ahead of time what the real question will be for everyone. Although he or she will ask decoy questions aloud, there can be an unspoken real question that the individual will assist participants to discover for themselves. This approach helps foster group discussions on a particular topic, or it might enable a therapist or counselor to help a client work through certain blocked issues.

Here is an example[4] in which the decoy questions are those spoken by the leader and heard by the participants, while the real question is kept in mind by the leader and is not revealed to participants until after the imagination portion of the exercise is completed:

1a) Decoy question spoken by leader: "In your imagination, see a book and describe it and your feelings about it. What does this book mean to you?"

1b) Real question, kept in mind by leader and/or written on a piece of paper: "See a book that symbolizes what the individual's life has been all about."

2a) Decoy question spoken by leader: "Open the book to a section. What is it you see, hear, feel, experience, or just somehow know?"

2b) Real question, kept in mind by leader and/or written on a piece of paper: "Let the individual have a personal message appropriate at this time."

3a) Decoy question spoken by leader: "See a structure. What do you see? This structure has a story to tell; what is it?"

3b) Real question, kept in mind by leader and/or written on a piece of paper: "Let the individual see a symbol of the thing that is most challenging in his or her life at this time."

4a) Decoy question spoken by leader: "See another structure. Now what do you see? This structure also has a story to tell; what is it?"

4b) Real question, kept in mind by leader and/or written on a piece of paper: "Let the individual see a symbol of the thing that is most *exciting* in his or her life at this time."

After being led through this exercise, a nineteen-year-old woman had the following experience:

The image that corresponded to my life story was a big blue fairy tale book that I had when I was a child. For me, the symbolism meant that my life story has been the enfolding tale of innocence, spirituality, and achieving expectations. I was also optimistic and had hope for the future.

---

[4] Based on an exercise formulated by Magaly del Carmen Rodriguez, *Creative Imaging Work*. Privately Published. 1988/89.

The section I turned to was a beautiful picture of the forest. My message is that I have a great deal of potential and possibilities. It can also suggest that I need to pay more attention to the small details in my life – being able to see the trees and the forest.

The first structure I saw was a large Japanese house with a heavy curved-style roof. It was beautiful and serene. Since this is a challenge, it seems to mean that right now I am trying to learn a lot of new information and foreign ideas (Japanese roof). I am in school and much of what I am studying is challenging, new and requires a lot of thought. At the same time, however, it has been a very serene and beautiful time of my life.

The second structure was a glass greenhouse. One of the things I may be most excited about is giving structure to the world of my hopes, dreams, imagination, and potential. I am also excited about showing my strengths and ideas to others.

As a final example, a woman in her fifties was led through a variation of the same exercise. In her experience, the participants were asked to see a book (life story), to turn to a section (personal message), to meet someone (an individual who can help answer the question), and to receive something from that person (a talent that the individual could utilize to solve his or her question). Here is her experience and what she learned from it:

The book I imagined was the Bible. That seemed appropriate since I have spent much of my life searching for spiritual insights that are relevant to me. The section I turned to was a picture of the inside a castle with no windows and no doors. This describes my life perfectly. I have material possessions, but I often feel imprisoned in a relationship (my marriage) that does not give me anything emotionally. As a couple we don't even have a dream for the future, we're just stuck in the "now" and don't see a way out.

I was really surprised to see my sister. In many ways I envy her life, her personality, even her marriage. She is such a spe-

cial person. To me this might mean that I have all of those same ingredients inside myself that my sister has. Somehow I just need to cultivate them in my own life.

When we were asked to imagine this person giving us something, my sister handed me a picture of her smile. Quite simply, I think it means that I need to have more joy in my life. Definitely true!

Maybe the whole thing suggests that I have been stuck in a rut and need to find a way out. I certainly need more joy. Maybe I can just imagine what my sister would do in my circumstance (or even ask her), and do likewise.

Conscious dreamplay accesses the subconscious mind's insights and intuition through the use of imagery and imagination. Just as in dreams, dreamplay symbols and images need to be interpreted, but this process again provides the individual with all manner of information. Conscious dreamplay is limited only by the imagination. Just as an individual can work with his or her dreams, obtaining countless insights into every area of life, conscious dreamplay can help access the mind's subconscious wisdom without the intermediary of sleep. Whether as a tool for personal guidance, as a means of clarifying an issue, as a method of obtaining information about one's self, or as a technique for glimpsing the future, the imagination game is a unique method of self-discovery.

Chapter Eight
Sample Dreamplay Images

(See Appendix 1 for possible interpretations.)

A. A woman in her twenties was asked to imagine a book (life story), a section (personal message), a first structure (challenge) and a second structure (something exciting).

I saw a brown-colored book like a diary. It was large and thick and seemed like it had been read a lot because it was worn.

When I opened the book to a section, I saw a sailboat. There were no words, just a beautiful scene with the boat sailing smoothly on the water.

The first structure I saw was the Tower of Babel and the second structure was a beautiful secluded beach house made of stucco (my boyfriend works with stucco).

B. Man in his forties was trying to decide between two vacation possibilities for his family. In order to get insights into the question, one door represented a camping trip; the other corresponded to a beach vacation. When doing the imagination exercise, he did not know which door applied to which vacation.

The first card I touched had the image of a very bright, white door. It had a gold doorknob and seemed very attractive. When I opened the door, I saw a mall with lots of different stores and people doing all kinds of things. There were movie theaters and restaurants. Everyone seemed to be having a good time. I rated the picture as an eight.

When I touched the second card, the door appeared to be the same at first. The door and the doorknob were just as attractive. However, when I opened the door I saw a gray concrete building. It was empty and stark and felt cold inside. I gave it a one.

When I turned over the questions, the first door corresponded to the beach vacation and the second door corresponded to the camping trip.

C. Woman in her fifties was asked to imagine a building (theme for next twelve months), people doing something in the building (activity occupying her time), a person standing out from the crowd (what individual should be personally involved with) and something just around the corner (unexpected surprise).

> *There was a big office building. It was very tall with lots of windows. When I looked inside the building, I could see that it was actually one of the largest laundromats I had ever seen. People were busy washing and dry cleaning and pressing all kinds of clothes. I noticed one woman sitting and sipping a cup of coffee while everyone else was working. For a minute she turned to look at a stack of dirty clothes, but she picked up a book and began to read it instead. When I imagined myself outside the building to see what was around the corner, I could see an amusement park.*

Conclusion

After more than twenty-five years as an interpreter of thousands of dreams, I can honestly say that I enjoy working with dreams and symbols more than ever before. It is still thrilling to discover the possible meaning of a personal dream or hear others exclaim, "Aha!" when they have been led to a probable meaning for themselves. I have also found the conscious dreamplay exercise to be a wonderful approach for helping individuals have "a dream," especially if they have difficulties remembering their dreams upon awakening. Dreamplay is not only a wonderful way to get insights into every imaginable question, it is also extremely helpful in enabling individuals to practice their interpretation skills.

Perhaps more than anything else, the wondrous insights available to us from the subconscious mind suggest that we are much more than our physical bodies. Consciousness is not limited to the body or to our perceptions of what we think we are. During the sleep-state, the mind becomes open to information from all space and time. This information ties into activities and events occurring in waking life and can be extremely helpful, if only the dreamer chooses to use it. This same type of information can be accessed through imagination games, intuitive imagery, or conscious dreamplay – tools that utilize the limitless boundaries of the imagination within the helpful parameters of personal insight and intuition.

For the most part, dreams contrast and correlate the events of the day, providing the individual with another look at the issues with which he or she is concerned. Dreams can provide an objective look at known facts, process potential solutions, or help acquire information and guidance not known or available to the conscious mind. Dreams address everything about an individual's life and wellbeing – physical, mental, and spiritual –

for dreams can relate to the health of the body, explore psychological issues and emotions, or even nurture the soul.

In all my years of working with dreams I have decided that if you want to work with your dreams, the most important element is practice. For that reason, you should start writing down your dreams immediately upon awakening. Although you may only remember a color, a scene, or a feeling, write it down. Even if you only have the feeling of a good night's sleep the next morning, write it down. If you remember seeing the face of someone you know, *write it down*. Let the subconscious mind know that you are serious.

If you wake up in the middle of the night, keep a "dream notebook" near your bed and write down a few scenes. You can write down the entire dream upon awakening the next morning. As you begin to write each morning, you will be surprised at how many dreams come to mind. You don't have to remember the entire story of the dream; what's important is the process of re-experiencing the experience.

People use several tricks to remember their dreams in the morning. You can tell yourself, "I will remember my dreams" when falling to sleep. Or you can drink a big glass of water in order to awaken in the middle of the night. You can also set the alarm to go off five to ten minutes earlier than usual. All these things can help dream recall. But whatever you do, keep practicing.

Whether an individual happens to be working with conscious dreamplay or dreams, remembering the meaning of a lot of symbols is not that important. Using a good dream dictionary, or even an unabridged dictionary, can be just as helpful as a list of memorized symbols. The theme or overall feeling of a dream, or some dreamplay imagery, is every bit as important as the symbols.

Since we know ourselves better than anyone else, ultimately, we are our own best dream interpreters. Our personal symbols take precedence over whatever anyone else might think of the symbolism. For that reason, it is a good idea to begin a "personal dream dictionary" and watch for reoccurring symbols, characters, themes, and emotions within our own dreams. Even when using conscious dreamplay to answer another individual's question, all symbolism should first be interpreted in terms of what the individual doing the imagining personally associates with that symbol.

Because other characters often become the subject of our dreams and imaginings, it is important to keep in mind that they usually symbolize something about ourselves. Even animals, nature, and inanimate objects can be symbolic for the individual. Since most dreams deal with the dreamer, we do not generally dream for other people unless we have specifically and consciously decided to do so – and even then, a dream will invariably have personal relevance.

Remember that there is more than one way to interpret a dream or conscious dreamplay exercise:

A) *Work with the theme first and the symbolism second.* Try describing the dream in no more than one or two sentences in terms of "What is happening to whom?" For many individuals, creating a possible story line for the images being portrayed is an easy way to decipher the meaning of a dream or imagery experience.

B) *Explore the emotional content of the dream or image.* Does it feel like a positive dream? A frustrating dream? A frightening dream? An inspiring dream? Remember that the emotion aroused by the dream or image generally corresponds to a situation or experience in your life that evokes a similar feeling or emotion.

C) *Determine whether the dream is literal or metaphorical, then interpret the symbolism accordingly.* Most dreams deal with personal, not global, events. Most dreams contrast and correlate the events of the day. What is it about the images portrayed that reminds the dreamer of his or her real life? A literal dream deals with some aspect of reality, while the same image in a metaphorical dream *symbolizes* something else. Dreams can be both metaphorical and literal.

D) *Attempt to analyze the dream in the light of your current life.* Dreams serve primarily as a means for your subconscious to wrestle with issues, concerns, or feelings that have been on your conscious mind.

E) *Work with symbol interpretation.* Buy a good dream dictionary (see "References and recommended reading" for list of resources) or an unabridged dictionary. Look up symbols that you already know and see whether or not the dictionary makes sense or agrees with you. Remember there should be a logical connection between a symbol and what it is supposed to mean. In other words, a dream does not mean something simply because someone says it does.

Using these approaches, anyone can begin working with his or her dreams immediately. Individuals can also begin playing the conscious dreamplay exercise for personal insights into virtually any question. Dreams, symbols, imagination, and the intuition can all work together to bring to the consciousness of individuals whatever they need to know in order to learn about themselves and to become all that they were meant to be.

As you begin to explore the depth of your own consciousness, finding insights into yourself, your life, and your relationships, you will be amazed at the depth of wisdom that has always been available to you in dreams and dreamplay. As you do so, you will be making a contribution to that day in the future when each and every individual is encouraged to work with dreams as a normal part of everyday life. I encourage and challenge you to begin exploring the wonderful world of symbolism, dreams, and intuitive imagery today.

Possible answers to end-of-chapter sample dreams and images

Chapter One:

A. A woman in her fifties has been extremely busy. The shelties mentioned in the dream had actually been dead for several years when this dream occurred:

> *I dreamed that I was inside my house and all of a sudden I remembered that I hadn't watered or feed my shelties in quite some time. For some reason, I had put them in a shed out back of the house and never went back to check on them. Suddenly, I was in a panic and tried to go and check on them but a neighbor showed up and kept interfering with me trying to go see my dogs. Finally, when the neighbor left I was able to go out to the shed. I was horrified to find that the dogs were gone!*

The fact that the dream occurs within the woman's house suggests that the dream is related to a current situation or experience. Her shelties may represent something she loves about herself, or something she loved about having the dogs in her life. Since the shelties have been in back of the house and essentially forgotten, perhaps the woman has been ignoring something important in her life. External demands keep vying for her attention. When she finally attends to this important matter, it is too late.

In real life, the woman was extremely busy with work, family and school obligations. She admitted that she had neglected herself the most.

She didn't take the time or feel that she had the time to do the things she loved. The dream encouraged her to rethink her priorities.

B. A woman in her forties, who is bothered by all the back-stabbing in her office, had the following dream:

> *I was speaking to the office receptionist about the fact that I was being promoted. I had decided that from now on there would be a new dress code that everyone would be wearing. I had on a smart-looking, business-type pantsuit to show her what I was talking about.*

The promotion in the dream suggests that the woman will be more prominent in some situation, probably having to do with work. The office receptionist may represent the act of communication. A dress code is symbolic of one's outer appearance, as well as one's demeanor, and the way an individual presents herself or himself to others. The fact that what the woman is wearing is in line with the proposed dress code can indicate that the dreamer knows how to interact well with others and knows how to fix problems. The dream may also indicate that the woman is literally going to be promoted and will be able to address the problems that arise in her new position.

C. This dream is by a middle-aged man who does not get along with his mother:

> *I dreamed that I was speaking to my mother and as I was speaking my two front teeth kept falling out. I'd push them back in but they kept falling out. The funny thing was, I don't think my mother noticed. It made me feel uncomfortable to be around her.*

The teeth falling out of the dreamer's mouth seems to indicate that he either does not feel comfortable speaking to his mother and does not really know what to say, or that things are coming out of his mouth that shouldn't be coming out, like gossip, for example. His mother does not see the problem. This suggests that either or both of them are oblivious to this communication problem. It might also be saying that the only time he speaks about his mother is behind her back. In real life, the dreamer felt that both interpretations were accurate.

Chapter Two:

A. An eighteen-year-old girl has this reoccurring dream. She has been trying to make changes in her life. About the chewing gum mentioned in the dream she says, "I do occasionally chew gum but only regular size pieces."

In the dream I am chewing a really big piece of gum. When I'm ready to take out the gum, it will not come out. In my attempt to remove the gum, it becomes stringy and sticks to my teeth. The gum never comes out!

A possible theme is that "Someone is having a hard time doing something." Another could be "Something is difficult to remove or change." Because the "sticky situation" is in the young woman's mouth, perhaps she is biting off more than she can chew or she is having a difficult time communicating. The dreamer admitted to being very frustrated with her life and with the fact that she was continually trying to make personal changes without success.

B. In real life, the husband of this woman in her forties has asked for a divorce. This is her dream:

I was working in a hospital. A man's wife was dying of lung disease. He and his son came to me and asked me to steal some medications for her. They kept telling me how she was suffering. I told them that I of all people understood but I could not steal drugs or bring in herbs that would interfere with her treatment. I also said there was a lot of security and I just couldn't do that. I reached over and got my stuff to leave and I was crying saying that I couldn't help them. I woke up crying.

The imagery is that "Someone or something is dying and apparently nothing can be done about it." Since the dreamer states that her husband has asked for a divorce, obviously it is the marriage that is dying; that's why the dreamer can understand the pain and suffering the man and his son are going through. The woman dying of a disease related to her chest probably symbolizes the dreamer's own broken heart. There does not appear to be anyone who can help. Because the dreamer is unable to provide medication in the dream, the woman has perhaps thought about "medicating" herself and has changed her mind, or she has come to realize that even such things as tranquilizers and alcohol will not help ease her pain.

C. A woman in her fifties is concern about her friend This is her dream:

> *I dreamed about going into a big house with one of my female friends. To our horror, in walking through the house there were all of these disembodied heads that we had to walk around just to get through to where we were going.*

Simply stated, "Someone is losing his or head over something." Since the dreamer is worried about a friend, the dream suggests that either the dreamer is losing her head in the situation, her friend is losing her head, or that both women are losing their heads. The house is symbolic of the current situation. Because the two women are walking around disembodied heads as they move through the house, it appears the dreamer is having a challenging time trying to figure how to move to help her friend with the problem.

Chapter Three:

A. A dreamer in her thirties complains of a relationship with her aggressive mother, a woman prone to critical comment.

I was going home and being followed by a Velociraptor dinosaur. I had reached home and the Velociraptor had followed me inside. I raced up the stairs and went into one of the rooms and shut and locked the door. Although the door was shut I knew the dinosaur would be breaking through the door at any moment. Afraid, I climbed out of the window and crawled out onto the roof of the porch that was below the window. I was kind of hanging below the roof so it wouldn't see me. It finally went away but I knew it would be back.

Next, my family was packing our belongings: the pets, the food, and the things that we needed quickly so we could leave and be safe from the dinosaur. The dream ended with my being able to watch the car, all packed up and loaded, with all of us inside, driving away

The mother's biting and aggressive temperament is represented by the Velociraptor dinosaur. The presence of the dinosaur inside the home suggests that the dreamer is either unable to escape her mother's criticism, or that her mother's criticism has become a part of the dreamer, making the dreamer critical of herself or others. Though the dreamer tries to escape the creature, she is unable to get away. This suggests that even if the dreamer is successful in avoiding her mother physically, the issues remain a part of her and need to be dealt with on their own. Even if the dreamer shuts out her mother, the problem will likely break into the dreamer's private thoughts. Being near the roof (thoughts) suggests that the woman has given some thought to dealing with this issue and has partially been successful ("It finally went away but I knew it would be back"), but there is still work to be done.

By driving away with her family, the dreamer is either able to escape her mother's criticism, or she is so caught up in her family's life that the issue is not prominent. However, overall the dream suggests that issues related to this relationship cannot be suppressed or avoided; something still needs to be done to resolve the effect the mother had, and still has, on her daughter.

B. A middle-aged man recalls a reoccurring dream that he often had as a teenager:

> *The dream is that I am at home in my parent's home where I grew up. All at once I look out the window and am frightened to see that a number of tornadoes are heading right for the property. Although afraid, I suddenly remember that this is something I have been through many times before. The thought comes to me that just as I have survived previously, I'll probably be able to survive this most recent storm. The last thing I remember is being afraid and simply hoping that I will be okay.*

Since the dream is a childhood dream, we can assume that it involves an issue that was relevant at the time. If the dream repeated itself in the present, it would probably indicate that a similar situation or experience was occurring in the man's life, rather than it being an unresolved issue related to that previous experience.

The parent's home represents his life, his surroundings, and perhaps even his personal security. Looking out the window at tornadoes suggests that he is observing some kind of volatile emotional upheaval. These arguments or outbursts are occurring around him, and are either something he participated in or was subjected to. However, since these repeated storms never injure him, we can assume that he has simply witnessed them rather than having been physically involved.

In real life, the dreamer admitted that his parents were always fighting during his youth. He stated that even though they fought behind their closed bedroom door, he could still hear their shouting through the walls. This really bothered him as a teenager and he hoped that it would stop. He wanted his parents to learn to get along. Eventually, however, the parents divorced.

C. A woman in her forties lives far from her family. Her elderly parents are still alive.

I was driving back to Iowa (where we use to visit my grandparents) with my Dad. We were going back to honor my great-great-grandfather. We finally drove into a dinky town in Iowa and drove up to a large house that looked almost like an office building or a courthouse. A crowd of people, Blacks and Whites, scattered about the lawn just staring. For some reason the scene seemed eerie.

I went into the house and was confronted by an angry lady who seemed to resemble me. She was irate and screamed at me for failing to visit my dying great-great-grandfather. She said that I could not see him any more and then she abruptly escorted me out of the house.

After a little reflection, I was determined to see him anyway because I had come a long way for that very purpose. I went back in the house and insisted on seeing him. Finally, the angry woman relented and led me back into the bedroom.

My great-great-grandfather was so old and aged and frail that I could hardly believe his condition. He was curled up in a fetal position and was as tiny as an infant. As I stood there looking at him in sadness, he opened his eyes as if to speak.

Suddenly, my alarm clock went off and I was awakened. I found myself desperately sad from the feeling of the dream and from my desire to know what he would have said to me.

The dream suggests that the woman is worried or concerned about a family issue or relationship. It is an important issue (office building/courthouse) but the dreamer does not know how to deal with it (people just standing around). She may also be worried or scared about the situation ("the scene seemed eerie").

Obviously, the angry woman is the dreamer herself who is upset over something. In actuality, that something is her father, who, the dream suggests, is a great, great, even grand individual. She apparently feels guilty about something related to her relationship with him. The dream represents her father as being very sick, very old, and even curled up in a fetal position. If he is ill or worried about something, then she feels guilty that she cannot spend more time with him, or she doesn't know what to do to help him, or both.

In real life, the dreamer expressed concern for her father and some measure of frustration that she did not get to spend as much time with him as she desired.

Chapter Four:

A. A female accountant in her forties dislikes male co-worker, "Bob."

> *I dreamed that I came to the office, and where my desk had once been, there was now a bed. Although I didn't seem surprised about it in the dream, Bob was waiting for me in bed. I smiled at him, took off my clothes and crawled in next to him and we started to kiss. I woke up feeling very confused and alarmed as to why I had done such a thing.*

Although the dreamer may be suppressing some unresolved sexual or romantic feelings, the dream is more likely about her work relationship with Bob. A bed where her desk should be suggests a partnership or cooperative venture of some kind, most likely with Bob. The project seems to go well and, to the dreamer's surprise, the two may even end up liking one another.

B. A mother is "very close" to her daughter, Amanda, who is about to attend an out-of-state college.

> *I was in the house and got a phone call that Amanda had been killed. The police were calling to tell me about her death. When I heard the news I screamed and dropped the phone. I ran through the house calling out to my husband, needing him to help me. I was horrified and sick to my stomach.*

Although this dream might have appeared precognitive, in speaking with the dreamer I discovered that the woman was about to "lose" her daughter to college. With this in mind, the dream is most likely about a mother's sadness and loss related to a child growing up and leaving home.

Because the two had been very close, the daughter departure for school may seem like a death; the old relationship is no longer alive. The woman's own higher self (police) is trying to make her deal with the change, indicating that perhaps the woman has been hesitant to talk about her fears, concerns, and sadness with anyone. The dream suggests that the woman needs to open up to her husband and release some of the anxiety and sadness that is making her sick to her stomach.

C. A woman is frustrated with her husband about their marriage; he is frustrated with his business partner about the company finances. This is the wife's dream.

> *I dreamed that I was standing in the dining room next to my husband, looking at my husband's business partner. I said to the partner that I didn't want anything to do with him because of how he had treated my husband. I no longer wanted to eat with him or be in the same room with him.*

Let's not assume that the dream is simply about the dreamer's relationship with her husband's business associate. Remember that most dreams deal with one's self. From a marital perspective, the dreamer is also her husband's "business partner." Being in the dining room suggests that there is an issue she has been dealing with (digesting) for quite some time. When the dreamer says that she no longer wants to have anything to do with the partner, does she mean the business partner or marriage partner?

In discussing the dream, the woman admitted that just as her husband was sick of dealing with his partner in business, she was sick of dealing with her husband. Rather than simply holding her thoughts within herself, the dream suggests that the woman needed to deal with her husband face-to-face, so that the two of them could resolve the situation.

Chapter Five:

A. A woman in her fifties is in the midst of life changes and needs to make decisions about her future.

> *I dreamt that there was an elegant looking woman who was standing by herself. She appeared calm and collected. Suddenly I noticed that she was missing her entire right arm. There wasn't even a stub where her arm should have been. I was carrying a white shawl at the time and I took it over to the woman and draped it around her shoulders. I don't know if I was trying to cover her missing arm or help her stay warm. She seemed appreciative and thanked me.*

Often, every character in a dream is symbolic of the dreamer. The elegant woman standing by herself suggests that the dreamer is regal and alone in real life. Although she may come across as stable, self-certain and self-sufficient, something has happened to make her feel as if she is missing a limb (suggestive of divorce or abandonment or great loss). Because it is her right arm and possibly symbolic of the future, perhaps something has been taken from this woman's future. In the dream, the woman, or her higher self, tries to comfort her and tell her that in spite of how things appear in the present, everything will be okay.

When the woman heard this interpretation, she replied, "That's it exactly!"

B. A twenty-year-old man has moved to a university town to attend school. He has not yet found a job and is worried.

> *I am trying to take a picture of an awesome sunset down a road. It gets better and better. The sky gets very cloudy with bright orange colors. As I try to take the picture, a little boy gets in the way. I keep hoping he will move but when he does the sunset is gone.*

The act of looking back down a road and taking a picture of a sunset is like reflecting upon your life and enjoying the memories that are fading (sunset). On the other hand, it could mean that something you have waited for can now be cherished and enjoyed, if it is not blocked by anything else.

Orange can be the color of creativity or sexuality. Because of current events in the dreamer's life, the color probably has something to do with a creative solution. The little boy might be symbolic of the dreamer's new life, or of his childish fears. In either case, the present situation is blocking, or interfering with, the dreamer's thoughts (clouds). Since the child does not get out of the way, perhaps the dreamer is having a difficult time coming to terms with the fact that his life has changed. Otherwise he is having difficulties facing his current problems.

The dreamer said that his inability to find work had caused him "to worry about everything." He added, "To me, the picture represented memories, experiences, and relationships. The sunset suggested the closing period of my life, a death. The dream seemed to say that childhood fears are either holding me back, or I am not moving past something."

C. A nineteen-year-old woman has developed romantic feelings for a male friend, Patrick, and is worried that the feelings will affect their friendship.

I had a dream that I was at a party. It seemed to be my house but it wasn't. I was outside and saw a snake in our neighbor's yard that looked like an anaconda. I went back in the house, found my friend Patrick, and told him about the snake. When we went outside to look for it, it wasn't there. Afterwards, we walked through another room leading outside to the front yard because he had to leave. On the way to Patrick's car, we passed some friends playing cards. Before he left, he kissed me on the cheek, then we hugged and he kissed me on the lips.

The next thing I remember was being at another house with another guy who is a friend. We are sitting on some monkey bars. Then I saw the snake again. This time it was winding itself around the pole and looping itself through the bars. I was scared but my friend told me it would be all right and wouldn't hurt me. Then Patrick came out (the other friend seemed to be gone) and we watched the snake go to the other yard.

The party suggests fun. In the process of having fun (in real life probably with her friend Patrick), the dreamer notices a snake, which can symbolize a male relationship or male sexuality. Because the snake is not in her yard, perhaps the dreamer really does not need to deal with it. Since she tells Patrick about the snake, she may have sexual feelings for him and may even have discussed the fact that her feelings extend beyond a mere friendship. However, when they look for the snake, it isn't there. This indicates that her feelings are not shared by Patrick, or that the two of them will have difficulty maintaining a sexual relationship. Patrick departure and other friends playing cards both suggest that the dreamer's relationship with Patrick is simply that of friends.

After the dreamer kisses Patrick she meets another friend; perhaps the dreamer has tried to find romantic relationship in other male friendships. This possibility is further reinforced because she and the friend are sitting on monkey bars, suggesting that they have been "monkeying around." As she monkeys around with her friend, the sexuality presents itself again. Once she and Patrick get together, the snake leaves.

In speaking with the dreamer, she explained that she planned to pursue a relationship with Patrick regardless of the dream's message. The dream imagery suggested a short-lived romance that would end in friendship. The dream might also be saying that, regardless of what transpired between them, there was nothing to fear as everything would work out okay. In this case the snake might represent fear of sexual expression; its leaving the yard once the two of them get together could indicate that the fear dissipates once they are romantically involved, or that the romance is over as soon as it begins.

Chapter Six:

A. A forty-three-year-old woman is interested in spiritual development and her personal mission in life.

> *I dreamed I was driving home in my Jeep. In real life, to get to my house on the mountain I have to drive up a very steep hill for about a half-mile, then wind around the mountain. On the steep hill, there were several boulders – all perfectly round and smooth. They were scattered randomly. I continued to drive. As I reached the first boulder I cautiously peered around it, saw*

the way was clear, and continued on to the next boulder. There were one or two other cars on the hill that were stopped and couldn't go any further. I managed to weave around all the obstacles by driving up to them slowly, looking for an open path, finding one, and continuing to drive. Eventually, I reached the top of the hill.

Since it is the dreamer who is driving her Jeep up the mountain to her house, perhaps the dream is about the woman's life journey, her search for spirituality, or both. The presence of boulders in her path suggests obstacles she will encounter (or has encountered) on her journey. The fact that the boulders are rounded and smoothed may mean that the dreamer has dealt with these issues for a long time, wearing them down in the process. Continuing her travels and cautiously planning her next move is perhaps symbolic of the dreamer's methodical decision-making process. Passing other cars on the road could represent leaving behind earlier problems, difficulties, or belief systems, or it might indicate surpassing her family's (or her personal) expectations. Reaching the top of the hill is associated with the achievement of personal and spiritual goals. Whether it is enlightenment or personal fulfillment she seeks, this woman is likely to succeed.

B. A young woman wants to return to college and focus on her career. Her husband is opposed to the idea and wants her to stay home with the kids.

I dreamed that I was walking along and noticed that a snake was biting my arm. I had to struggle to get it off my arm. Later, as I was walking, I noticed that a snake (could have been the same one) was biting my ankle.

A snake can mean male energy or temptation. Because of current events in the woman's life, it appears as though a snake bites her arm as she travels her life's journey (walking along). The arm can symbolize the self, or it can be associated with free will. Biting can correspond to negative words. The imagery suggests that a male energy is trying to interfere with her free will, either physically or verbally. The snake biting her ankle also suggests that a male energy is trying to impede her path.

In real life, the woman decided that the dream illustrated her relationship with her husband. She decided that both a family and a career were important to her and she ignored her husband's attempts to prevent her from returning to college.

C. This man complains of feeling tired and lethargic and has trouble concentrating.

> *I dreamed that I was crazy and having problems thinking. Somehow I was able to look inside my head. With my skull open, I could see all kinds of gears and wheels spinning around in their proper place, except for one. One of the wheels had stopped running altogether because a particle of dirt or trash had gotten stuck in it.*

The imagery of the head suggests that the man's condition may be due to his own thoughts or some kind of a physical block. His lethargy and concentration problems may be due to depression, repressed anger, hopelessness, or feeling "stuck" in a routine. If the condition is purely physical, then the logical assumption is that the dreamer is having problems with his physical elimination processes (the piece of trash getting stuck), causing the toxins to build up in his system, which in turn results in both a lack of energy and slow thought-processes.

Chapter Seven:
A. A woman in her forties who works at a bank in Norfolk, Virginia, had this dream:

> *I saw Norfolk, Virginia from the air. I could see the naval shipyard and downtown. Suddenly a missile descended from the sky and struck the ground near the waterside. Before anyone could realize what had happened, the city was annihilated and an enormous mushroom cloud rose high up into the air.*

Because of Norfolk's national importance as a naval shipyard, the woman feared the dream was precognitive and wanted to know how she could warn the city. She also wondered how it would affect the safety of those outside the city. During our conversation I learned that her husband was not in the Navy, that she did not associate her family with Norfolk, but that she did work in Norfolk. So the dream probably had to do with the end of her job. Though I never heard from the woman again, several months later Norfolk was hit by a series of bank mergers and acquisitions that affected numerous employees.

B. A thirty-year-old man was close to his grandfather, who died six weeks before this dream:

> *A few weeks after my Grandfather died, I began having a reoccurring dream about him. In the dream there was some kind of a large family gathering like Thanksgiving. Everyone was gathered around the table in the kitchen for dinner. I happened to look through the door that led into the living room and saw my Grandfather, who I knew was dead, sitting on the couch all by himself. I was the only one who could see him. I went and sat by him on the couch and started talking with him.*
>
> *My grandfather told me that he was all right and doing just fine. He also thanked me and stated that he had really enjoyed being my grandfather. He gave me a hug and we talked some more. The experience was very uplifting and yet the whole time the rest of my family remained completely oblivious to my grandfather's presence and just went on with their dinner.*

Since consciousness is not confined to the physical body, it is likely that a real communication occurred between the dreamer and his grandfather. In other words, the grandfather was simply trying to reassure his loved ones that he was doing well, even though he was no longer physically alive.

In conversation with the dreamer, I learned that he was the only one in his family who ever paid any attention to his dreams, which sheds some light on the repetitive nature of the dream. In all likelihood the grandfather was trying to reassure the family that he was fine; all the individuals at the dinner table were probably contacted in the dream-state. But since only the thirty-year-old paid any attention to his dreams, the rest of the family remained oblivious to the grandfather's reassuring message.

C. A man in his sixties wrote out the question, "What do I need to work on spiritually?" before going to sleep. This dream followed:

> *I dreamed that I was in the army (I have never been in the army) and I was some kind of a drill sergeant doing important paperwork. My desk was filled with important papers and things that were scheduled – everything was neatly organized and in their proper place. Suddenly a younger man came into my office unannounced. He was singing and dancing and appeared to be having a very good time with himself. To my surprise, he jumped up on top of my desk and started tap dancing all over my paperwork. Everything that I had neatly organized was in disarray. After making a thorough mess, the man continued to sing and dance right out of my office. Immediately, I picked up the phone and called security and yelled into the received, "I want that man arrested, and I want to know who he is!" I slammed the phone down, very angry for the interruption. Suddenly, security came into my office bringing the man who had caused the disruption. They announced that they had caught him and that he was "the company clown."*

Although the dreamer had never been in the armed services, he had regimented habits. Although retired, his entire schedule was structured hour-by-hour; he adhered religiously to his "to do" lists that he kept. The dreamer's wife had repeatedly encouraged him to relax, but to no avail. Only after receiving this dreams guidance that he even realized he had a problem. The dream finally convinced him to have fun and take things less seriously.

Chapter Eight:

A. A woman in her twenties was asked to imagine a book (life story), a section (personal message), a first structure (challenge) and a second structure (something exciting).

> *I saw a brown-colored book like a diary. It was large and thick and seemed like it had been read a lot because it was worn.*
> *When I opened the book to a section, I saw a sailboat. There were no words, just a beautiful scene with the boat sailing smoothly on the water.*
> *The first structure I saw was the Tower of Babel and the second structure was a beautiful secluded beach house made of stucco (my boyfriend works with stucco).*

It is remarkable that the woman saw a diary in the dream; she was unaware that the book she imagined symbolized her "life story." The book's brown color suggests a practical and down-to-earth nature, and is perhaps descriptive of the woman herself. The book's thickness and worn look could represent the woman's many life experiences, in spite of her age.

The sailboat is a personal message for her. It suggests that the present is a beautiful and serene time for her, or that she needs to try and incorporate beauty and serenity into her life right now. The sailboat image may also represent a spiritual journey.

The Tower of Babel is a phallic symbol, suggesting a male energy. Because of the Biblical account, it also symbolizes communication problems. It is interesting to note that in real life the woman and her boyfriend were having difficulties communicating, especially about their future together.

Her association of stucco with her boyfriend suggests that what she was most excited about is the future (one filled with serenity and perhaps even spiritual interests) that she is planning with him.

B. Man in his forties was trying to decide between two vacation possibilities for his family. In order to get insights into the question, one door represented a camping trip; the other corresponded to a beach vacation. When doing the imagination exercise, he did not know which door applied to which vacation.

The first card I touched had the image of a very bright, white door. It had a gold doorknob and seemed very attractive. When I opened the door, I saw a mall with lots of different stores and people doing all kinds of things. There were movie theaters and restaurants. Everyone seemed to be having a good time. I rated the picture as an eight.

When I touched the second card, the door appeared to be the same at first. The door and the doorknob were just as attractive. However, when I opened the door I saw a gray concrete building. It was empty and stark and felt cold inside. I gave it a one.

When I turned over the questions, the first door corresponded to the beach vacation and the second door corresponded to the camping trip.

Since both doors appeared identical at first, both vacations looked just as fun to him at the beginning. But obviously the image behind the first door is much more appealing. The mall imagery might correspond to the fact that there will be plenty to do at the beach (lots of activities) and every member of his family will have a good time. On the other hand, the second door suggests boredom, the lack of excitement, or the possibility of weather problems during the camping trip – after all, it was "cold" in the building.

C. Woman in her fifties was asked to imagine a building (theme for next twelve months), people doing something in the building (activity occupying her time), a person standing out from the crowd (what individual should be personally involved with) and something just around the corner (unexpected surprise).

There was a big office building. It was very tall with lots of windows. When I looked inside the building, I could see that it was actually one of the largest laundromats I had ever seen. People were busy washing and dry cleaning and pressing all kinds of clothes. I noticed one woman sitting and sipping a cup of coffee while everyone else was working. For a minute she turned to look at a stack of dirty clothes, but she picked up a

book and began to read it instead. When I imagined myself
outside the building to see what was around the corner, I could
see an amusement park.

The imagery fits a woman who is very busy putting things in order, or "cleaning up" something related to her home, work, or life in general. The woman sitting and relaxing might be a hint that the dreamer also needs to take the time to relax and enjoy herself, regardless of how busy she is. The need for relaxation and personal enjoyment is further reinforced by the image of the amusement park. It could be that something fun is just around the corner.

Conscious dreamplay, relaxation and additional exercises

Relaxation Exercise

(A relaxation reverie is spoken at about one-third the normal rate of speech.)

Become comfortable and relaxed and begin focusing your attention on your breathing. Let your awareness begin to notice how cool the air feels as you inhale and how warm it feels as you breathe out. After a few moments, bring your attention to your feet and ankles. Breathe in relaxation to your feet and ankles, and breathe out any tension.

Next, breathe in relaxation to your legs and knees, and breathe out any tension there. Breathe in relaxation to your hips, thighs, and buttocks, and breathe out any tension.

Move up to your back, stomach and chest. Breathe in relaxation to these areas, and breathe out any tension. Next, breathe in relaxation to your shoulders and neck, breathe out any tension.

Breathe in relaxation to your head and forehead. Let got of any tension there. Take a deep breath and simply relax.

Conscious Dreamplay Exercise I

(To help participants gain insights into an unknown question)

1) Decoy question: "Imagine a package or a present of any kind."
[Pause.] "How does this package appear to you?"

2) Decoy question: "Unwrap your package and see what's inside."
[Pause.] "How do you feel about what you see?"

3) Decoy question: "Snap your fingers and what happens to the contents
inside?" [Pause.] "Now, how do you feel about what you see?"

Conscious Dreamplay Exercise II

(To help participants gain insights into an unknown question)

1) Decoy question: "Imagine a door." [Pause.] "What does it look
like to you?"

2) Decoy question: "Open the door and see what's behind it." [Pause.]
"What do you see and how do you feel about it?"

3) Decoy question: "Imagine it is six months from now?" [Pause.] "What
happens to the image behind the door?"

Conscious Dreamplay Exercise III

*(For a group leader to guide participants in perceiving their
lives over the next year)*

1a) Decoy question spoken by leader: "In your imagination, see a
building." [Pause.] "What is it you see, hear, feel, or experience?"

1b) Real question, kept in mind by leader and/or written on a piece of
paper: "See a building that symbolizes the theme of the individual's next
twelve months."

2a) Decoy question spoken by leader: "There are people inside the
building. What are they doing?"

2b) Real question, kept in mind by leader and/or written on a piece of paper: "Give a visual representation of what activities will be occupying most of the individual's time."

3a) Decoy question spoken by leader: "Someone in the building seems to stand out to you. Who is this individual and what is that individual doing?"

3b) Real question, kept in mind by leader and/or written on a piece of paper: "Is there an activity that the individual should make certain to incorporate into daily life?"

4a) Decoy question spoken by leader: "There may be something wonderful just around the corner from the building." [Pause.] "If so, what is it?"

4b) Real question, kept in mind by leader and/or written on a piece of paper: "Is the individual about to be surprised by something? If so, picture it."

More than 350 common dream symbols and their possible interpretation

Symbol/Image:
Possible Interpretations Include:

Accident
1. Suggests a problem or a dangerous situation.
2. Could correspond to a warning.

Actor/Actress
1. One who plays a part.
2. May represent aspects of self. See also Self.
3. Whatever we associate with that individual. See also People.

Advisor
1. Can correspond to one's higher self.
2. May be associated with personal advice or counsel. See also People.

Airplane
1. May be associated with a spiritual journey.
2. A lofty idea or project.
3. Might correspond to one's present direction or journey.
   See also Automobile.

Alarm Clock
1. Corresponds with timing.
2. May be associated with a warning or a message.

Alien
1. A foreign idea, experience or circumstance.
2. Depending on the imagery, might be associated with one's higher or lower self, or one's dreams or fears. See also People.

Alligator
1. Might represent biting words or a rough exterior.
2. See also Animals.

Ambulance
1. Suggests an emergency situation.
2. Could represent a serious concern or message.
3. See also Automobile.

Amusement Park
1. Associated with joy, fun, happiness or relaxation. See also Places.
2. Could suggest the need to relax and have fun, or that one was not taking something seriously.

Angel
1. A heavenly messenger.
2. Associated with spirit.
3. See also People.

Animals
1. Suggests whatever is associated with that animal.
2. Symbolic of the creature's most outstanding trait or appearance (e.g. a lamb could indicate innocence or purity; a giraffe might represent a strong will because of the animal's neck; a turtle could be long life or slow and methodical behavior; an elephant could suggest memory or being nosey, etc.)

Ants
1. That which is biting or bugging me. See also Bugs.
2. Could represent a busy worker or someone who feels insignificant.

Arm
1. Associated with self. See also Self.
2. May be symbolic of free will. See also Body.
3. Metaphorically, to keep at arm's length = to keep at a distance.

Arrow
1. Can correspond to a weapon or a message.
2. Might symbolize a male energy. See also Phallus.

Atomic Bomb
1. A dangerous or explosive situation.
2. Something which may cause a problem or annihilation.
3. Might be associated with an emotional experience.

Attic
1. Could indicate the higher mind, the higher self, or one's own thoughts.
2. May correspond to memories or the subconscious.
3. See also House.

Automobile/Car
1. Often associated with one's direction or one's present journey.
2. Might be symbolic of the physical body or one's health (e.g. engine = heart; exhaust = eliminations, etc.).

Baby
1. Associated with a new beginning, project, idea or relationship.
2. May represent a real pregnancy.
3. See also People.

Back
1. Metaphorically, it's in back of me = behind me; to turn one's back = to ignore.
2. See also Body.

Backyard
1. Could represent a present situation or experience. See also Yard.
2. Can be associated with things in the past.
3. See also House.

Banana
1. Can be a real dietary suggestion. See also Food.
2. Might be associated with male sexuality. See also Phallus.
3. Might correspond to one who monkeys around. See also Monkey.

Bank
1. Symbolic of money, finance or success.
2. See also Building.

Barefoot
1. Not being prepared for something, being exposed, or being vulnerable.
2. Could indicate relaxation.
3. See also Feet.

Basement
1. May be associated with the unconscious or repressed feelings and desires.
2. See also House.

Basket
1. Associated with one's personal belongings, talents, or that which one controls or can draw upon.
2. Might correspond to receptivity or female energy. See also Womb.

Bathroom
1. Corresponds with eliminations or the need to eliminate something.
2. See also House.

Bear
1. Can be angry, ferocious, overprotective, overbearing, or dangerous. See also Animal.
2. Metaphorically, a real bear = a difficult person;
   a bear market = stocks in decline.

Bed/Bedroom
1. Associated with a relationship or sexuality.
2. Metaphorically, to be in bed with something = to be involved.
3. See also House.

Bee
1. That which bites or stings (e.g. words spoken). See also Bugs.
2. Metaphorically, busy as a bee = extremely productive.

Beetle
1. That which is irritating. See also Bugs.
2. An Egyptian scarab corresponds to good luck or fortune.

Bible
1. Associated with spiritual truths or insights.
2. Could represent a spiritual journey.
3. Might correspond to one's soul or Akashic record. See also Library.

Bicycle
1. A solitary journey or experience.
2. A balancing act.
3. Could represent one's physical body.

Bird
1. May represent a message or a messenger.
2. See also Animals.

Birdcage
1. Can be symbolic of confinement. See also Bird.
2. May represent one's personal association with birdcages.
3. Might symbolize that which has one confined or imprisoned. See also Prison.

Black
1. Corresponds to the unknown. See also Colors.
2. Might be symbolic of depression or death. See also Death.

Blanket
1. Can be associated with personal security or warmth.
2. Depending on the imagery, might indicate protecting one's self emotionally.
3. Could represent sexuality or a relationship. See also Bed/Bedroom.

Blue
1. Can correspond to spirituality or higher wisdom.
2. Metaphorically, feeling blue might represent feeling sad.
3. See also Colors.

Boat
1. A spiritual or an emotional journey. See also Water.
2. May indicate one's present situation or experience.

Bomb/Bombing
1. An explosive or volatile situation.
2. Could be a warning of a possible problem or a negative situation.
3. Metaphorically, dropped a bomb = said something that had major repercussions.

Body
1. Associated with the self. See also Self.
2. May symbolize whatever we associate with that body part (e.g. one's feet could indicate direction; one's face may be associated with self-esteem; one's mouth could represent words spoken; reaching for something with one's fingers or arms could symbolize free will, etc.)

Book
1. Corresponds to knowledge or insight.
2. Might symbolize one's soul or Akashic record. See also Library.
3. Metaphorically, by the book = according to regulations.

Box
1. Associated with a self-contained experience or idea.
2. That which one has under control.
3. Could represent female sexuality. See also Womb.

Brakes
1. Corresponds with the need to stop or slow down.
2. See also Automobile.

Bread
1. Sustenance or food. See also Food.
2. Metaphorically, bread = money.

Bridge
1. That which allows a transformative passage.
2. Associated with bridging a new experience, understanding or insight.

Briefcase
1. Corresponds to one's personal identity or occupation.
2. Might be related to that which is "in hand" (e.g. that with which one is already involved).
3. Associated with what one has on his or her mind.

Brother
1. May represent the individual or whatever trait or character we most associate with that person.
2. Can be symbolic of our relationship with that person. See also People.

Brown
1. Corresponds to the material, the earthy, the practical.
2. See also Colors.

Bugs
1. May be symbolic of whatever is associated with that bug (e.g. mosquitoes suck one's life, a butterfly corresponds to transformation, etc.)
2. That which is biting, irritating, or bugging me.

Building
1. Corresponds to whatever we associate with that building (e.g. a post office = a message; a church = spirituality; an office building = work, etc.).
2. May be symbolic of self or one's present situation or experience. See also House.
3. A tall building could correspond to male sexuality. See also Phallus.
4. An opened or a receptive portion of a building might correspond to female sexuality. See also Womb.

Bull
1. That which is stubborn or aggressive. See also Animals.
2. Metaphorically, bull = nonsense; a bull market = stocks on the rise.
3. May represent primal urges and desires.

Bus
1. Can correspond to a group journey, project, situation, or experience.
2. See also Automobile.

Butterfly
1. Often associated with personal transformation and change.
2. Might correspond to a spiritual experience or journey.
   See also Bugs.

Cake
1. Corresponds to a celebration or recognition.
2. Metaphorically, to have your cake and eat it too = to get everything you desire.

Cancer
1. A problem or a situation that is eating away at the self.
2. Might indicate the need to see a doctor.

Candy
1. That which is sweet, tempting or desirable.
2. Might indicate the need to change one's dietary habits.

Canyon
1. May correspond to a separation, a divide, or a disagreement in an experience or a relationship.
2. Might be symbolic of female sexuality. See also Womb.

Captain
1. Associated with a higher authority or power (e.g. God, one's boss, one's father, one's spouse, etc.).
2. See also People.

Carpet
1. Symbolic of one's foundation. See also House.
2. Metaphorically, being called on the carpet = getting into trouble.

Cartoon
1. Can correspond to a creative, unbelievable, humorous, or unreal situation.
2. Might be associated with one's present experience.

Castle
1. Can correspond to one's personal experience, situation, or physical body. See also House.
2. Associated with protective walls from the outside world (e.g. insulated by one's own emotions).

Cat
1. Corresponds to whatever one may associate with cats. See also Animals.
2. Depending upon personal association, may be symbolic of independence, love, contentment, or allergies.
3. A black cat could symbolize bad luck.

Cave
1. That which is hidden, concealed, or unconscious.
2. Could be indicative of female sexuality. See also Womb.
3. Might correspond to the lower self.

Chicken
1. Metaphorically, to be a chicken = to be afraid.
2. See also Animals.

Child
1. A young project, experience or idea.
2. Associated with one's inner child. See also People.

Church
1. Often represents spirituality or faith.
2. Can be associated with whatever one has previously experienced with churches. See also Building.

Circumcision
1. Could correspond to feeling emasculated or personally challenged. See also Phallus.
2. Might represent coming of age.
3. Can be symbolic of a promise or a covenant.

Clock
1. Suggestive of timing for a situation or an experience.
2. Could indicate the present, past, or future.

Clothing
1. Associated with one's outer self, physical body, or identity.
2. The type of clothing is often symbolic of what is being portrayed (e.g. a hat = ideas, shoes = direction, overcoat = emotions, etc.)
3. See also Historical Clothing/Settings.

Clouds
1. Can correspond to ideas, emotions, or the weather.
2. See also Sky.

Clown
1. Can be associated with joy, foolishness, or frivolity.
   See also People.
2. Might represent the display of one's emotions.
3. Metaphorically, a clown = foolish or inept.

Coat
1. May be associated with that which insulates self from the world
   e.g. emotions).
2. Could indicate present situation or experience. See also Clothing.

Coffin
1. Corresponds to great change or the end of something.
2. Associated with death. See also Death.

Colors
Black = May be associated with unconsciousness, negativity, or depression.
Blue = Often associated with spirituality or higher wisdom.
Metaphorically, feeling blue might represent feeling sad.
Brass = Can represent a false or tarnished truth.
Brown = Corresponds to the material, the earthy, the practical.
Gold = Can correspond to that which is invaluable (spiritually or materially), or that which is of the Divine.
Gray = Related to confusion, depression, or that which is cloudy or unclear.
Green = May be symbolic of healing, growth, or envy.
Indigo = Often associated with the higher mind or the soul.
Ivory = Somewhat clouded from the truth; may relate to detachment and aloofness.
Orange = Associated with creativity, energy, or sexuality.
Pink = Symbolic of higher or divine love, health ("in the pink").
Purple = Can be related to spiritual development or a regal nature.
Red = Symbolic of sexuality, anger or rage; also associated with base creativity.
Silver = Often associated with material value or intuition.
Violet = Corresponds to great spirituality or spiritual dedication.
White = Associated with purity, innocence, and holiness.
Yellow = Represents intelligence or personal power.

Compass
1. Associated with direction.
2. Could symbolize one's life journey.

Compost
1. That which is rotten or decaying.
2. Could symbolize the need for or the act of something being recycled.

Condom
1. Associated with male sexuality. See also Phallus.
2. Could correspond to being vulnerable or personal protection (sexual, emotional, or otherwise).

Counselor
1. Can represent one's higher self. See also People.
2. Indicative of personal counsel.

Court
1. Associated with a higher authority or power.
2. Could represent feeling judged, tried, criticized, or condemned.

Cowboy
1. Can correspond to whatever one may associate with cowboys (e.g. independence, freedom, warfare, etc). See also People.
2. Metaphorically, a real cowboy = really independent, or really cocky and unmanageable.

Crayon
1. Associated with creativity and personal talent.
2. See also Colors.

Crucifix
1. May be symbolic of faith.
2. Might correspond to that which is crucifying self or causing self to suffer.

Crystals
1. Corresponds to clarity or insight.
2. Could represent one's dreams, ideals, or goals.

Dancing
1. A joyful or harmonious journey. See also Music.
2. Might represent a relationship or a cooperative venture.

Death
1. Associated with change, transition, or the end of an experience.
2. Could indicate feelings of being overwhelmed by a situation.
3. Might represent death.
4. Dreams of the dead can correspond with real communication.

Defecate
1. To eliminate, dispose, or release something.
2. To spoil or ruin.

Devil
1. Corresponds to temptation, hidden desires, one's shadow, or evil.
2. Associated with temptation.
3. Might be symbolic of one's own fears.
4. Could symbolize a male energy. See also People.

Diary
1. Represents one's life story.
2. Could correspond to one's soul or Akashic record. See also Library.

Dishes
1. That which is being presented (e.g. ideas or experiences).
2. Washing dishes could symbolize cleansing a situation.

Doctor
1. Can be associated with physical, emotional or spiritual health. See also People.
2. Could indicate a higher authority or power.
3. Metaphorically, to doctor something = to change or take care of it.

Dog
1. Corresponds to whatever one may associate with dogs. See also Animals.
2. May represent friendship, love, or companionship.
3. Depending upon imagery may represent anger and aggression, or a situation to which one is allergic.

Dolphin
1. Associated with spirituality or higher intelligence.
2. See also Animals.

Door
1. Can correspond to new opportunities or directions. See also House.
2. The location and appearance of the door will have a great deal to do with its possible symbolic meaning (e.g. front door = something coming to face you; a locked door = that which doesn't want to be dealt with, etc.).

Dove
1. A messenger of peace and tranquility.
2. May represent whatever one associates with doves. See also Animals.

Eagle
1. Associated with a message of idealism or strength.
2. See also Animals.

Ear
1. Corresponds with listening or the need to be heard.
2. See also Body.

Earth
1. Represents one's current situation or experience.
2. Can indicate stability.

Eating
1. Associated with choices or decisions made (e.g. free will).
2. That which one takes into one's self. See also Food.

Eiffel Tower
1. May be symbolic of love, romance, passion, or travel.
2. Can represent a male figure or energy. See also Phallus.
3. See also Tower.

Eight
1. May correspond to balance, good judgment, infinity, great strength, or great weakness.
2. See also Numbers.

Elephant
1. Can be symbolic of memory, age, wisdom, or power.
2. Could represent that which is "nosey" or that which is "thick-skinned."
3. See also Animals.

Elevator
1. Corresponds to different levels of consciousness.
2. The ups and downs of one's present experience.
3. Ascending might signify that which is a promotion; descending might indicate a demotion.

Eleven
1. Represents mastery in the physical dimension; might also indicate two.
2. See also Numbers.

Emotions
1. Whatever emotion is being portrayed often indicates a real-life situation in which the dreamer feels the very same emotion.

Enemy
1. Represents that from which one is running or avoiding in self, or in others.
2. Can be symbolic of something that causes one to be fearful.
3. See also People.

Engine
1. Can be symbolic of that which gives power and vitality.
2. Might be associated with one's heart.
3. Depending upon imagery, see also Automobile.

Eyes
1. Associated with vision or insight.
2. An aspect of self. See also Body.
3. Might be indicative of the all-seeing Eye (e.g. God).

Face
1. Corresponds to the self. See also Body and Self.
2. How self may be viewed by others.
3. That which one is currently facing. See also People.

Fairy
1. Associated with magic or enchantment.
2. Could represent a spiritual messenger. See also People.
3. Metaphorically, a fairy = a person who is gay;
   a fairy tale = an untruth.

Falling
1. Symbolic of a situation that is out of control or overwhelming.
2. Corresponds to a fear of failing or a loss of personal power/will.

Father
1. May represent the individual or whatever trait or character we most associate with that person.
2. Associated with a higher authority or power (e.g. God, one's boss, one's father, one's spouse, etc.).
3. Can be symbolic of our relationship with that person. See also People.

Feet
1. Associated with one's direction or life's journey. See also Body.
2. Could indicate one's foundation or understanding.

Fence
1. That which confines or protects.
2. May be associated with one's current situation or experience.
3. Metaphorically, on the fence = being undecided.

Fiancé/Fiancée
1. Corresponds to a cooperative venture or relationship.
2. Could indicate personal integration.

Fight
1. Symbolic of a personal struggle with self or others.
2. That with which one is at-war. See also War.

Fingers
1. Represents choice or free will.
2. An extension of self. See also Body.

Fire
1. Can represent strong emotions or anger.
2. That which destroys or purifies.
3. Metaphorically, playing with fire = taking a big risk.

Fish
1. Often associated with spirituality or faith.
2. Metaphorically, something's fishy = something's not right; a fish out of water = that which is out of place or inappropriate for the situation.
3. See also Food.

Fishbowl
1. Associated with one's spiritual belief system. See also Fish.
2. May be associated with one's present situation or experience.

Five
1. Associated with change, the five senses, new beginnings, or will power.
2. See also Numbers.

Flag
1. A signal, a message, or an affiliation.
2. Associated with whatever country or image is being portrayed.
3. Can correspond to patriotism.

Flood
1. Represents an overwhelming emotional experience or situation. See also Water.
2. Can indicate personal transformation and change.

Flowers
1. Symbolic of one's talents or abilities.
2. That which is about to blossom or bloom.
3. Different types of flowers are often associated with different meaning (e.g. a lily can correspond to rebirth, a rose is suggestive of love, etc.).

Flying
1. Can be associated with great joy or euphoria.
2. May correspond to an elevating experience or spirituality.
3. Suggests personal mastery or rising above an experience.

Flying Saucer
1. That which is a foreign idea, experience, or circumstance.
2. Depending on the imagery, might be associated with one's dreams or fears.
3. See also Airplane.

Fog
1. Symbolic of personal confusion or doubt.
2. Might suggest conflicting emotions.

Food
1. May indicate a real dietary suggestion (e.g. something one needs to eat or something one needs to stop eating).
2. That which one takes into one's self.
3. Can be associated with free will.
4. Associated with physical, mental, or spiritual sustenance.

Forehead
1. Associated with an idea, thought, or decision in the forefront of one's mind.
2. See also Head.

Forest
1. One's present situation or experience.
2. Can indicate growth and stability or overgrowth and confusion.
3. Metaphorically, can't see the forest for the trees = getting caught up in details.
4. See also Trees or Woods.

Fountain
1. Associated with spiritual knowledge or insight. See also Water.
2. The fountain of youth represents youth and vitality.
3. Could indicate the bursting forth of talents, emotions, ideas, or sexuality.

Four
1. Can correspond to the earth, materiality, service, stability, or human love.
2. See also Numbers.

Four Leaf Clover
1. Associated with good luck or good fortune.
2. See also Four.

Friend
1. Corresponds to the individual's outstanding character, talent, or trait. See also People.
2. An aspect of self in relationship to that individual.
3. Can be symbolic of our relationship with that person.

Front
1. Metaphorically, it's in front of me = ahead of me; to be up front = to be direct.
2. See also Body.

Front Yard
1. Could represent present situation or experience. See also Yard.
2. Can be associated with that which is in the future.
3. See also House.

Funeral
1. Corresponds to great change or the end of something.
2. Associated with death. See also Death.
3. In portions of South America, symbolic that someone is about to get married.

Garage
1. Symbolic of personal storage (e.g. memory)
2. Can represent one's self. See also Automobile and House.

Garbage
1. That which has been discarded or needs to be discarded.
2. Might correspond to something worthless or immoral.

Genie
1. The magical or limitless part of one's self. See also People.
2. Associated with magic, power, or boundless creativity.
3. Could represent a wish or a lucky situation.

Ghost
1. May symbolize the past, one's shadow, or that which is haunting you.
2. See also Death.

Giant
1. That which appears large, threatening, or immense. See also People.
2. Might correspond to an obstacle or a challenge.

Giraffe
1. May be symbolic of one's neck (e.g. sticking one's neck out) or will power.
2. See also Animals.

Glasses
1. Corresponds to vision, comprehension, or insight.
2. That through which one perceives. See also Eyes.

Gloves
1. That which covers one's hands. See also Hands.
2. Metaphorically, to handle with kid gloves = to be careful with.

God
1. Associated with the Creator, the ultimate spiritual source, and the impetus behind all that exists.
2. Might correspond to one's higher self. See also People.

Gold
1. Might symbolize spiritual wealth, insight, or information.
2. Associated with one's own potential talents or resources.

Gold (color)
1. Can correspond to that which is invaluable (spiritually or materially), or that which is of the Divine.
2. See also Colors.

Grandfather/Grandmother
1. May represent the individual or whatever trait or character we most associate with that person. See also People.
2. Often corresponds with wisdom or insight.
3. Might be symbolic of an aspect of our relationship with that individual.

Grass
1. Can represent one's current situation or experience. See also Yard.
2. Depending on the imagery, might be associated with growth and vitality.
3. Metaphorically, grass = marijuana.

Grave
1. Corresponds to great change or the end of something.
2. Associated with death. See also Death.
3. Could represent that which one has buried or repressed.

Gray
1. Related to confusion, depression, or that which is cloudy or unclear.
2. See also Colors.

Green
1. May be symbolic of healing, growth, or envy.
2. See also Colors.

Gun
1. Can represent violence, aggression, or dominance.
2. May be symbolic of a male energy. See also Phallus.

Hair
1. Often related to thoughts, ideas, or insights. See also Body.
2. Metaphorically, a hair-raising experience = a scary experience; splitting hairs = to argue about the trivial.

Hammer
1. Can correspond to a powerful or driving force.
2. That which builds or creates.
3. Might be associated with a male energy. See also Phallus.

Hand
1. Associated with the self or one's free will. See also Body.
2. Metaphorically, to give a hand = to congratulate; to force one's hand = to push someone to action.

Hat
1. Often related to thoughts, ideas, or insights. See also Hair.
2. Might indicate one's occupation or that with which one is involved.

Hat Pin
1. Can correspond to thoughts, ideas or insights. See also Hat.
2. Might be associated with something that is stuck or pricking at one's thoughts.

Head
1. Can correspond with the self or one's thoughts. See also Body.
2. Metaphorically, losing one's head = not thinking something through; using one's head = giving something much contemplation.

Hero
1. May represent one's inner talents or higher self. See also People.
2. The qualities of strength, perseverance, and determination.

Hill
1. A small challenge, obstacle or goal. See also Mountain.
2. May be associated with levels of ability or consciousness.
3. Metaphorically, over the hill = past one's prime.

Historical Clothing/Settings
1. Often corresponds with whatever an individual associates with that clothing or setting. See also Clothing.
2. May indicate a past-life memory pattern that is similar to a present-day experience.
3. See also Places.

Horse
1. Can be associated with a message or a messenger. See also Animals.
2. Might represent one's sexuality or desire.
3. Metaphorically, to horse around = to be not serious.

Hospital
1. Symbolic of a problem, situation, or health concern requiring immediate attention. See also Building.
2. That which needs to be healed or is in the process of being healed.

Hotel
1. Associated with a temporary experience or situation. See also House and Building.
2. Might correspond with whatever an individual associates with hotels.

House/Rooms in House
1. Represents one's personal experience or current situation.
2. Rooms in a house can correspond to whatever is associated with that room (e.g. Master Bedroom = relationships or sexuality; kitchen = diet or home and family; bathroom = eliminations.
3. A house can also represent one's physical body (roof or attic = thoughts, basement = unconsciousness, etc.). See also Self.

Hurricane
1. Often symbolic of emotional turmoil.
2. Can be associated with a challenging experience or situation over which one has no control.

Husband
1. Might correspond to a partnership or a cooperative venture. See also Marriage or Wedding.
2. May represent the individual or whatever trait or character we most associate with that person.
3. Can be symbolic of our relationship with that person. See also People.

Ice
1. Associated with frozen, chilly, or repressed emotion. See also Water.
2. Metaphorically, on thin ice = on dangerous ground.

Indian
1. Might correspond to nature, the earth, or whatever one associates with Indians.
2. Could symbolize a spiritual journey or quest. See also People.

Indigo
1. Often associated with the higher mind or the soul.
2. See also Colors.

Insects
1. May be symbolic of whatever is associated with that bug (e.g. mosquitoes suck one's life, a butterfly corresponds to transformation, etc.)
2. That which is biting, irritating, or bugging me.

Island
1. Can correspond with one's present situation or experience.
2. Symbolic of an emotional or spiritual experience. See also Water.
3. Might represent one who is isolated or set apart.

Ivory
1. Somewhat clouded from the truth; may relate to detachment and aloofness.
2. See also Colors.

Jail
1. That which has one caged, or a captive (e.g. work, a situation or a relationship, etc.).
2. Represents a confining experience. See also Building.

Jaws
1. Might be associated with words spoken. See also Teeth.
2. A clenched jaw could be indicative of something being held inside.
3. Might correspond with one's self and image. See also Face.

Jewels
1. Symbolic of one's talents or abilities.
2. Might be associated with truth, wisdom, healing, or insight.
3. Metaphorically, a real jewel = something valuable.

Jungle
1. Could represent one's present situation or experience.
2. That which is lush, overgrown, or filled with life and potential.
3. Metaphorically, it's a jungle out there = the situation is wild and uncontrollable.

Key
1. Associated with the solution or the answer.
2. Metaphorically, to hold the keys = to hold the answer or the power.

Kidnapped
1. Corresponds to that which is taken or stolen.
2. Associated with something being out of one's control.

King
1. Associated with a higher authority or power (e.g. God, one's boss, one's father, one's spouse, etc.).
2. See also People.

Kiss
1. Suggestive of affection, passion, sexuality, or friendship.
2. May correspond to a cooperative venture or situation.

Kitchen
1. Associated with diet or home and family. See also House.
2. That which one is preparing or taking into one's self.

Kitten
1. May be symbolic of love, comfort, or security. See also Cat.
2. See also Animals.

Knife
1. Can represent anger, aggression, or power.
2. Might suggest that which cuts or divides.
3. May symbolize a male energy. See also Phallus.

Ladder
1. Corresponds to different levels of consciousness.
2. The ups and downs of one's present experience.
3. Ascending might signify a promotion whereas descending might indicate a demotion.
4. Walking under a ladder could represent an unlucky situation or experience.

Lake
1. Can correspond to a spiritual or an emotional source. See also Water.
2. That which is at peace or tranquil.

Lamb
1. Represents purity, innocence, or meekness. See also Animals.
2. Metaphorically, as innocent as a lamb = extremely gentle.
3. Biblically, might represent the Christ. See also People.

Lamp
1. Can be symbolic of light or illumination.
2. Might correspond to placing a focus or an insight on a situation or experience.
3. A genie's lamp is symbolic of good luck. See also Genie.

Lawn
1. Can represent one's current situation or experience. See also Yard.
2. Depending on the imagery, might be associated with growth and vitality.
3. Metaphorically, grass = marijuana.

Leaves
1. Associated with growth, possibilities, or new ideas.
2. Blowing leaves may indicate something discarded or the passage of time.

Leeches
1. That which drains one's energy or life force.
2. Could correspond to an individual who is using another.

Left
1. Associated with the past.
2. Might correspond to the left brain or logic.

Legs
1. Often symbolic of one's direction or present standing. See also Body.
2. Could represent one's foundation or support system.

Letter
1. Represents a message or a communication.
2. Information from another source (e.g. one's intuition, another person).

Library
1. Can be associated with knowledge, learning, or insight. See also Building.
2. Could correspond to one's own soul or Akashic record.

Light
1. Associated with a flash of insight or a new idea.
2. Can correspond to spiritual truths or insight.
3. Might represent God or one's higher self.

Lightning
1. An emotional storm or outburst.
2. Symbolic of a warning message.
3. Might indicate vivid flashes of insight or ideas.

Lion
1. Represents personal power. See also Animals.
2. The king of the forest (e.g. the boss, one's higher self, etc.).
3. Might be symbolic of a play on words or one who is lying.

Liquor
1. Can be associated with over-indulgence or a loss of personal inhibitions.
2. Might be symbolic of "the spirits" (e.g. spirituality or emotion).

Living Room
1. One's present situation or experience. See also House.
2. The environment in which one finds herself or himself (e.g. work, home, a relationship, etc.).

Lottery
1. Often associated with good luck or good fortune.
2. Might be literal and symbolic of chance and one's personal timing.

Luggage
1. Associated with one's own baggage (e.g. feelings, beliefs, talents or problems).
2. Could represent a real or metaphorical trip (e.g. a vacation or traveling between thought, ideas, or goals).
3. Might correspond to memory.

Mail/Mail Carrier
1. Represents a message or a messenger.
2. Information from another source (e.g. one's intuition, another person).
3. If a mail carrier is being portrayed, see also People.

Mall
1. Symbolic of choices, opportunities, decisions, or personal activities.
2. Can correspond with whatever one may associate with a mall. See also Places.

Man
1. Can indicate the masculine side of one's self or another. See also Phallus.
2. Could be associated with masculine traits (e.g. strength, courage, stubbornness, etc.).
3. See also People.

Marriage
1. Represents a partnership, a new venture, or a relationship.
2. Could indicate a cooperative situation or experience.
3. Might be a real marriage.
4. Associated with coming to terms with another.

Milk
1. Might indicate a real dietary suggestion. See also Food.
2. That which nurtures or feeds one's self.
3. Can be associated with one's own mother. See also Mother.

Mirror
1. Reflective of the self or the situation.
2. Could frame things in an alternative perspective.
3. Might be associated with memory and personal reflection.
4. Breaking a mirror might correspond to an unlucky situation or experience.

Money
1. Symbolic of money, finance, or success.
2. Could represent energy or personal power.

Monkey
1. Might correspond to one who monkeys around. See also Animal.
2. May represent foolishness or pranks.

Monster
1. Can represent one's fears or problems. See also People.
2. That from which one is running.

Moon
1. Associated with the emotions and the intuition.
2. Can correspond to the feminine aspects of one's self.
3. See also Womb.

Mother
1. May represent the individual or whatever trait or character we most associate with that person.
2. Associated with a higher authority or power (e.g. God, one's boss, one's father, one's spouse, etc.).
3. May be symbolic of our relationship with that person. See also People.

Mountain
1. Represents a goal, a challenge, a destination, or an accomplishment.
2. May be associated with higher mental or spiritual states of awareness.
3. Ascending a mountain might indicate a promotion; falling off a mountain might indicate a failure.

Mouth
1. Corresponds to words spoken or that which takes into one's self. See also Body.
2. Metaphorically, having a big mouth = speaking too much.
3. See also Teeth.

Movies
1. Can correspond to one's life story, present situation, or soul's journey.
2. Could be symbolic of whatever one associates with that movie. See also Actor/Actress.

Mud
1. An emotional or unclear situation or experience.
2. A hindrance, an obstacle, or that which has created a problem (e.g. a muddy situation).

Music
1. Associated with a harmonious situation or experience.
2. See also Dancing.

Nail
1. Symbolic of that which holds things together.
2. Might be associated with crucifixioon. See also Crucifix.

Naked
1. Corresponds to showing off or vulnerability.
2. Might represent the act of becoming completely exposed.

Neck
1. Often corresponds to the personal will. See also Body.
2. Metaphorically, putting one's neck out = taking a chance; wring one's neck = to punish.

Newspaper
1. A message.
2. Associated with knowledge, insight, or information.

Nightmares
1. A situation or experience from which one has been running.
2. May be associated with that which one has ignored or neglected.
3. Can correspond to fears or personal anxieties.

Nine
1. Can represent fulfillment, completion, transformation, or wholeness.
2. See also Numbers.

Nose
1. Associated with the self or one's personal identity. See also Self and Head.
2. Can correspond with a sense of smell.
3. Metaphorically, led by the nose = easily manipulated; being nosey = being involved where one shouldn't.

Numbers

Zero = Symbolic of nothing, that which is absent or the all-encompassing.

One = The first, the beginning, individuality; personal survival.

Two = Can symbolize duality, opposites, relationships; sexuality.

Three = Represents body, mind, spirit; the trinity; great strength or personal power.

Four = Can correspond to the earth, materiality, service, stability, or human love.

Five = Associated with change, the five senses, new beginnings, or will power.

Six = Can indicate symmetry, beauty, and harmony; human dominance or Christ-mindedness.

Seven = Might be associated with spirituality, sacredness, perfection, or the seven spiritual centers/chakras.

Eight = May correspond to balance, good judgment, infinity, great strength or great weakness.

Nine = Can represent fulfillment, completion, transformation or wholeness.

Ten = Can suggest completeness and strength; or, the same as One.

Eleven = Represents mastery in the physical dimension; might also indicate two.

Twelve = Can correspond to cosmic order, the circle of life; or same as three.

Thirteen = Bad luck; same as four.

Twenty-two = Mastery in the mental/emotional dimension; same as four.

Thirty-three = Mastery in the spiritual dimension; same as six.

Forty = Associated with cleansing, purification, trial, or transformation; same as four.

Nurse
1. Can be associated with physical, emotional, or spiritual health.
2. Might represent one's higher self. See also People.
3. Metaphorically, to nurse something = to take care or it.

Ocean
1. An emotional situation or experience. See also Water.
2. Associated with a spiritual journey.
3. Might represent one's own unconscious or subconscious mind.

Office
1. Symbolic of work. See also Building.
2. One's present situation or experience.
3. A duty or an obligation.

Old Person
1. May correspond to wisdom or one's Higher Self.
2. See also People.

One
1. The first, the beginning, individuality; personal survival.
2. See also Numbers.

Orange (color)
1. Associated with creativity, energy, or sexuality.
2. See also Colors.

Orange Juice/Oranges
1. Might indicate a real dietary suggestion and the need for vitamin C.
2. See also Food.

Osteopath
1. Corresponds to the spine, literally or metaphorical (e.g. the need for a physical adjustment or one's personal power and self-esteem).
2. Can be associated with health. See also People.
3. Could indicate a higher authority or power.

Owl
1. Associated with wisdom. See also Animals.
2. Metaphorically, a night owl = one who stays up late.

Pants
1. Can correspond to one's direction. See also Legs.
2. Might be associated with one's personal identity or belief system.
3. Metaphorically, wearing the pants in the family = being the boss.

Parachute
1. Symbolic of escaping or deserting a situation.
2. Can indicate a descent.
3. Metaphorically, a golden parachute = a generous severance package.

Parents
1. Associated with a higher authority or power (e.g. God, one's boss, one's father, one's spouse, etc.).
2. May represent the individuals or whatever trait or character we most associate with them.
3. May be symbolic of our relationship with that person.
See also People.

Paris
1. Can correspond to a romance, good food or a vacation.
2. Associated with whatever one thinks of Paris.

Party
1. Represents a party or a celebration.
2. A message of congratulations or recognition.

Pen/Pencil
1. Associated with ideas, words, or experiences.
2. Indicative of communication.

Penis
1. Associated with male energy. See also Phallus.
2. Might be associated with sexuality. See also Sex.
3. Could indicate one who is oversexed or repressing sexuality.

People
1. Generally represents various aspects of oneself, or aspects of self in relationship to that individual.
2. Symbolic of faults, virtues, or activities that we associate with that individual.
3. Famous people are generally symbolic of their outstanding characteristics or talent.
4. Female people can represent female traits and abilities.
See also Womb.
5. Male people can represent male traits and abilities.
See also Phallus.

Phallus
1. May symbolize a male or masculine energy. See also Man.
2. Can correspond to male sexuality.
3. The positive masculine traits of one's self or another (e.g. logical, determined or persevering).
4. The negative masculine traits of one's self or another (e.g. selfish, tactless or aggressive).

Pig
1. Can correspond with greed, filth, selfishness, or gluttony.
2. See also Animals.

Pink
1. Symbolic of higher or divine love. See also Colors.
2. Metaphorically, in the pink = having good health.

Places
1. Corresponds to activities occurring in that locale:
   old workplace = work; old home = homelife;
   school = learning experience; library = knowledge;
   cleaners = that which needs cleansing, etc.
2. Some historical settings can correspond to a literal past-life memory. See also Historical Clothing/Settings.
3. See also Building.

Pocket
1. Associated with one's personal belongings, talents, or that which one controls or can draw upon.
2. Might correspond to receptivity or female energy. See also Womb.

Poison
1. Represents that which is deadly, dangerous, or making one sick.
2. Can symbolize a harmful experience that is occurring.

Police
1. Associated with one's higher consciousness, the law, or one's higher self.
2. That which provides legal and moral guidelines. See also People.
3. Could represent one who is in control (e.g. the boss, God).

Post Office
1. Represents a message or a communication.
2. Information from another source (e.g. one's intuition; another person).
3. See also Building.

Pregnant
1. Symbolic of a new beginning, a new project, a new relationship, or a new situation.
2. Might represent a real pregnancy.

President
1. Associated with a higher authority or power (e.g. God, one's boss, one's father, one's spouse, etc.).
2. See also People.

Priest
1. Can be symbolic of a spiritual presence, messenger, or authority.
2. Might indicate one's own higher self.
3. See also People.

Prison
1. That which has one caged or captive (e.g. work, a situation or a relationship, etc.).
2. Represents a confining experience. See also Building.

Psychic
1. Can be associated with intuition or one's higher self. See also People.
2. Could be symbolic of insight or a message.

Purple
1. Can be related to spiritual development or a regal nature.
2. See also Colors.

Purse
1. Symbolic or money, finance, or success.
2. Associated with one's identity, energy, or personal power.
3. Could correspond to female sexuality. See also Womb.

Pyramid
1. Symbolic of initiation, transformation, or esoteric information.
2. Can correspond with whatever one may think of places with pyramids (e.g. Egypt or Mexico).
3. Might be associated with real travel.

Queen
1. Associated with a higher authority or power (e.g. God, one's boss, one's father, one's spouse, etc.).
2. See also People.

Rabbit
1. Can correspond to sexuality or pregnancy.
2. Because of the ears, could be associated with listening.
3. See also Animals.

Radio
1. May be symbolic of transmitting or receiving a message or information.
2. Associated with tuning to higher levels of awareness or intuition.

Rain
1. Often corresponds to an emotional experience or outburst. See also Water.
2. Might be associated with a physical, mental, or spiritual cleansing.
3. Metaphorically, raining on a parade = dampening the enthusiasm.

Rainbow
1. Often associated with good luck or good fortune.
2. Might indicate a promise or a covenant.
3. May be symbolic of the end of a stormy experience.

Rake
1. Might correspond with gathering something together.
2. Symbolic of that upon which one is working.

Rape
1. Can represent an abusive situation or experience.
2. Corresponds to brutality, anger, and aggression. See also Fight.
3. May be a warning of being violated, abused, or taken advantage of.

Rat
1. Associated with one who is evil, cruel, sneaky, or intimidating.
2. See also Animals.

Raven
1. Can be associated with a messenger of ending, bad luck, or death. See also Death.
2. See also Animals.

Red
1. Symbolic of sexuality, anger, or rage; can also be associated with base creativity.
2. See also Colors.

Restaurant
1. Where one is being fed or nurtured. See also Building or Food.
2. Could represent one's present situation or experience.
3. Might be symbolic of one's dietary habits or thoughts.

Right
1. Associated with the future.
2. Might correspond to the right brain or intuition and emotion.

River
1. Associated with the flow of emotion, spirit, or intuition. See also Water.
2. Can correspond to one's life journey or the passage of time.

Road
1. Often represents one's present journey or experience.
2. Metaphorically, being at the crossroads = being faced with a choice or decisions.

Rocks
1. Symbolic of difficulties, obstacles, problems, or life's stumbling blocks.
2. Can represent hardened emotions or stubborn immobility.
3. Worn and smooth rocks could correspond to being worn down by life's experiences.
4. Metaphorically, on the rocks = having great difficulty, or being served with ice.

Roof
1. Can correspond with one's thoughts or ideas. See also House.
2. Might be associated with spirituality, intuition, or personal security.
3. That which covers one's present situation or experience.

Room
1. Symbolic of aspects of one's self.
2. Can correspond with whatever is associated with that room (e.g. master bedroom = relationships; basement = unconsciousness, etc.).
3. See also House.

Rooster
1. Associated with a self-certain or a cocky male. See also Phallus.
2. Can be symbolic of a message or messenger of timing. See also Animals.

Rose
1. Symbolic of love or relationship.
2. Can correspond with one's talents or abilities. See also Flowers.

Run
1. Often associated with what one is running from (e.g. self, a present situation, one's own fears, etc.).
2. Might correspond to the race of life.

Salt
1. Could correspond to a real dietary suggestion.
2. Metaphorically, the salt of the earth = that which is the best or the finest.

Scar
1. A problem, worry, or situation one is currently facing.
2. A past wound or memory affecting the present.
3. Whatever part of the body being scarred may have significance (e.g. face = self; legs = direction; head = thoughts, etc.).

School
1. Corresponds to a present learning situation or experience. See also Building.
2. Can be symbolic of that which one is experiencing.
3. Associated with what is being learned from, or taught to, others.

Scissors
1. Might represent the end of or a separation from an experience. See also Death.
2. Can be associated with cutting or injurious words or actions.

Self
1. Associated with one's individuality, traits, abilities or shortcomings.
2. Can be symbolic of what one needs to work on.
3. See also People, Man or Woman.

Seven
1. Might be associated with spirituality, sacredness, perfection, or the seven spiritual centers/chakras.
2. See also Numbers.

Sex
1. Corresponds to sexuality, reproduction, relationships, or self-gratification.
2. Can be associated with being oversexed or repressing one's sexual desires.
3. Symbolic of what one has been ignoring or overlooking (i.e. a sex dream can cause one to remember the experience).
4. Might represent creativity or energy.
5. Could indicate a partnership or a cooperative venture.
6. See also Phallus or Womb.

Shadow
1. Can correspond to one's shadow side. See also Self.
2. That which is only partially revealed or understood.
3. The projection of one's problems unto others. See also People.
4. Might be symbolic of memory.

Shampoo
1. Associated with changing or cleansing one's thoughts.
2. Can be symbolic of getting something or someone out of one's head.
3. Might represent dwelling upon a thought or an activity.

Sheets
1. Can be associated with sexuality or a relationship. See also Bed/Bedroom.
2. Depending on the imagery, might indicate vulnerability or protecting one's self emotionally.

Shirt
1. Associated with one's outer self, physical body, or identity. See also Clothing.
2. Metaphorically, wearing one's shirt on his/her sleeve = being overly emotional.
3. Can be symbolic of one's outer appearance, thoughts, personal experience, or occupation.

Shoes
1. Often associated with one's present direction or foundational under standing. See also Feet.
2. Metaphorically, being in someone else's shoes = attempting to understand another's experience;
   filling someone else's shoes = taking another's place.

Shopping
1. Can correspond with free will, choices, and decisions.
2. See also Building.

Sister
1. May represent the individual or whatever trait or character we most associate with that person.
2. May be associated with an aspect of our relationship with that person. See also People.

Six
1. Can indicate symmetry, beauty, and harmony; human dominance or Christ-mindedness.
2. See also Numbers.

Sky
1. Associated with spirituality, thoughts, ideas or insight.
2. The condition of the sky determines the meaning (e.g. a sunny sky can mean a bright or positive experience; a cloudy sky could be associated with a variety or worries or problems, etc.).
3. Metaphorically, the sky is the limit = all kinds of possibilities.

Skyscraper
1. Often symbolic of one's work. See also Building.
2. As a phallic symbol, may correspond to a male energy. See also Phallus.

Smoke
1. Can correspond with a message or a signal.
2. Could be associated with a lack of clarity.
3. Metaphorically, something is up in smoke = something is ruined.

Snake
1. Often associated with male energy or sexuality. See also Phallus.
2. Can represent temptation or evil. See also Animals.
3. Might indicate the creative energy of the kundalini.
4. Could be associated with healing (e.g. the caduceus).

Snow
1. Can correspond to repressed or frozen emotions. See also Ice.
2. Associated with an experience or situation left out in the cold.
3. See also Water.

Spider
1. Can represent that which is biting or bothering. See also Bugs.
2. May be symbolic of one who is attempting to entrap or ensnare.
3. Might indicate one who is spinning a web of deception.

Stage
1. Corresponds to one's present situation or experience.
2. That which one is currently perceiving.

Statue
1. That which is solid or unmoving. See also People.
2. Could indicate one who is emotionally detached, or one who is upon a pedestal.
3. Might represent a prize or an honor.

Statue of Liberty
1. Associated with freedom, independence, or liberty.
2. Might correspond to new beginnings. See also Statue.

Sun
1. That which lights one's experience or warms one's way (e.g. God, spirituality, an experience, an idea, another person, etc.).
2. Associated with a pleasant experience or idea.
3. Can correspond to the masculine aspects of one's self.
4. See also Phallus.

Swim
1. A spiritual or emotional journey or experience. See also Water.
2. That into which one is presently submerged.

Sword
1. Associated with aggression or dominance. See also Phallus.
2. Can correspond to that which cuts, injures, or divides.

Teacher
1. Symbolic of an authority figure or one's higher self.
   See also People.
2. Associated with what is attempting to be learned from,
   or taught to, others.
3. Can correspond to a present learning situation or experience.

Teeth
1. Teeth can be symbolic of words (e.g. that which is in one's mouth).
2. Teeth falling out is often related to things coming out of one's
   mouth that shouldn't (e.g. gossip).
3. Different types of teeth suggest different meanings
   (false teeth = false words; baby teeth = immaturity, etc.).
4. See also Mouth.

Telephone
1. Associated with a message or communication.
2. Might indicate receiving information, insight, or intuition from
   another source.

Telescope
1. Can correspond to clarity of vision.
2. Represents the ability to see that which is far off (e.g. the future).
3. Associated with the close inspection of an experience or activity.
4. Might indicate giving things more scrutiny than is necessary.

Television
1. Can correspond with one's present situation or experience.
2. Associated with a message or communication.
3. Might indicate the receipt of information, insight, or intuition.

Temple
1. Often represents spirituality or faith.
2. Can correspond with whatever one may associate with temples. See also Building.
3. May be indicative of a past-life memory pattern that is similar to a present-day experience. See also Historical Clothing/Settings.

Ten
1. Can suggest completeness and strength; or, the same as One.
2. See also Numbers.

Tent
1. Suggests a temporary experience or situation. See also House.
2. Might correspond to nature, the earth, or whatever one associates with Indians. See also People.

Three
1. Represents body, mind, spirit; the trinity; great strength or personal power.
2. See also Numbers.

Throat
1. Often associated with one's free will.
2. Can correspond to the voice or one's ability to communicate.
3. Metaphorically, to cut one's throat = to destroy someone; shoved down his throat = to force him.

Toilet
1. Corresponds with eliminations or the need to eliminate something.
2. See also House.

Tornado
1. Often symbolic of emotional turmoil.
2. Can be associated with a challenging experience or situation over which one has no control.

Tower
1. Can represent a male figure or energy. See also Phallus.
2. May be associated with a lofty idea or experience. See also Building.
3. Might be indicative of one who is emotionally isolated and withdrawn.

Train
1. Associated with a life journey.
2. Can correspond with one's present situation or experience.
3. Might represent a new destination or travel.
4. See also Automobile.

Trees
1. Associated with growth and vitality. See also Forest.
2. Different types of trees have different meaning (e.g. an apple tree could represent the need to see a doctor, or personal temptation; a willow tree could indicate the need to bend in the face of a challenging experience, etc.).
3. Metaphorically, can't see the forest for the trees = one who gets caught up in details and is unable to see the entire experience.

Trolls
1. Corresponds to something that diverts one from a path or direction.
2. That which can steal innocence. See also People.

Tunnel
1. Associated with one's personal journey or with other levels of consciousness.
2. Might be associated with a female figure or energy. See also Womb.
3. Could be indicative of the unconsciousness or memory.
4. Metaphorically, light at the end of the tunnel = positive things are on their way.
5. Might be associated with death or transition. See also Death.

Turtle
1. Can be associated with a long life, or that which is slow and methodical.
2. May be symbolic of that which withdraws into its shell. See also Animals.

Twelve
1. Can correspond to cosmic order, the circle of life; or same as Three.
2. See also Numbers.

Two
1. Can symbolize duality, opposites, relationships; sexuality.
2. See also Numbers.

Uniform
1. Can correspond to occupation, present situation or state of mind.
2. Suggestive of one who falls in line or follows orders.
3. See also Clothing.

Vagina
1. Associated with female energy. See also Womb.
2. Might be associated with sexuality. See also Sex.
3. Could indicate one who is oversexed or repressing sexuality.

Violet
1. Corresponds to great spirituality or spiritual dedication.
2. See also Colors.

Vulture
1. Associated with death and decay. See also Death.
2. Metaphorically, a vulture = one who preys upon another.
3. See also Animals.

Walk
1. Can correspond to one's present direction or experience.
2. May be symbolic of the journey of life.

Wall
1. That which prevents someone or something from going in or out.
2. May be representative of a barrier or limitation.
3. Metaphorically, he's like a wall = he's emotionally closed off.

Wallet
1. Symbolic of money, finance, or success.
2. Associated with one's identity, energy or personal power.
3. Could correspond to male sexuality. See also Phallus.

War
1. Can correspond to a physical or emotional conflict or confrontation.
2. Symbolic of a personal struggle with self or others.
3. Often associated with a current situation or experience.

Wash
1. That which needs to be cleansed, purified, or released.
2. Metaphorically, to wash one's hands = to relinquish responsibility; all washed up = completely ruined.
3. See also Water.

Watch
1. Associated with timing.
2. See also Clock.

Water
1. Associated with spirituality and the emotions.
2. Might represent a spiritual or emotional journey or experience.
3. Can indicate insight, intuition, or the unconscious.
4. Might be symbolic of metaphorical associations
   (e.g. making one's mouth water = a strong desire for;
   being in hot water = being in trouble).
5. May represent a physical or emotional release.

Waterbed
1. Associated with a relationship or sexuality. See also Bed/Bedroom.
2. Might correspond to an emotional situation or experience.
   See also Water.

Wedding
1. Represents a partnership, a new venture, or a relationship.
2. Could indicate a cooperative situation or experience.
3. Might be a real wedding.
4. Associated with coming to terms with another.

Whale
1. Can represent a large situation or experience. See also Animals.
2. Might be associated with repressed emotions.

White
1. Associated with purity, innocence, and holiness.
2. See also Colors.

Weeds
1. Can correspond to problems or a situation that needs to be dealt
   with.
2. Associated with the unwanted.
3. May be symbolic of obstacles that need to be removed.

Wife
1. Might correspond to a partnership or a cooperative venture. See also Marriage or Wedding.
2. May represent the individual or whatever trait or character we most associate with that person.
3. Can be symbolic of our relationship with that person. See also People.

Wind
1. May be associated with an emotional situation or experience.
2. Depending upon imagery, see also Hurricane or Tornado.

Window
1. Can correspond to the perception of new possibilities or opportunities.
2. Associated with clarity and insight, or personal reflection.
3. See also House.

Witch
1. Associated with a female energy or influence. See also People.
2. Can represent magic, the enchanted, or the mysterious.
3. Could indicate one who is bewitching or charming.
4. See also Woman.

Woman
1. Can indicate the feminine side of one's self or another. See also Womb.
2. Could be associated with feminine traits (e.g. emotional receptivity, intuition, cooperation, etc.).
3. See also People.

Womb
1. May symbolize a female or feminine energy. See also Woman.
2. Can correspond to female sexuality.
3. The positive feminine traits of one's self or another (e.g. empathetic, patient or intuitive).
4. The negative feminine traits of one's self or another (e.g. moody, critical or possessive).

Woods
1. One's present situation or experience.
2. Can indicate growth and stability or overgrowth and confusion.
3. Metaphorically, not out of the woods = there are still problems.
4. See also Trees or Forest.

Wrist
1. Can be associated with the self or one's free will.
2. See also Body.

X-ray
1. Can correspond with the ability to see through an obstacle, a situation, a person or an experience.
2. Associated with clarity of vision.
3. Might indicate the need to take a closer look at something.
4. See also Eyes.

Yard
1. Associated with one's current situation or experience.
2. That which needs to be addressed, dealt with, or taken care of.
3. You may also wish to see House.

Yellow
1. Represents intelligence or personal power.
2. See also Colors.

Zebra
1. Can represent the act of seeing things black and white.
2. Associated with a messenger. See also Horse
3. See also Animals.

Zero
1. Symbolic of nothing, that which is absent, or the all-encompassing.
2. See also Numbers.

Zoo
1. Associated with untamed aspects of one's self, one's environment or an experience.
2. Metaphorically, this place is a zoo = this place is filled with confusion and chaos.
3. See also Animals.

References and recommended reading

Cayce, Edgar (readings). *Dreams and Dreaming. Volumes I and II.* Association for Research and Enlightenment, Inc.: Virginia Beach, Virginia. 1974, 1976.

Gottlieb, Annie and Slobodan D. Pesic. *The Cube...Keep the Secret.* HarperSanFranciso: San Francisco. 1995.

Pehrson, John B. and Susan E. Mehrtens. *Intuitive Imagery: A Resource at Work.* Butterworth-Heinemann: Boston. 1997.

Rodriguez, Magaly del Carmen. *Creative Imaging Work.* Privately Published. 1988/89.

Tanner, Wilda B. *The Mystical, Magical, Marvelous World of Dreams.* Sparrow Hawk Press: Tahlequah, Oklahoma. 1988.

The Jewish Encyclopedia. Funk and Wagnalls: London. 1901.

Todeschi, Kevin J. *The Encyclopedia of Symbolism.* Perigee Books: New York. 1995.

Van de Castle, Robert L. *Our Dreaming Mind.* Ballantine Books: New York. 1994.

Webster's New Universal Unabridged Dictionary. Simon & Schuster: New York. 1979.